ABOUT THE AUTHOR

Dr. Luis Leal, born in Mexico, was educated in this country (Ph.D., University of Chicago, 1950), of which he is a citizen. He is now Professor of Spanish American literature at the University of Illinois, Champaign-Urbana, where he has been since 1959. He is the author of over one hundred literary articles and several books, as well as contributions to the *Encyclopedia Britannica* on Latin American writers, among them Mariano Azuela. His latest books are: a complete history of the Spanish American short story *(Historia del cuento hispanoamericano,* 1966), a survey of contemporary Mexican literature published by the Pan American Union *(Panorama de la literatura mexicana actual,* 1968), and an anthology of contemporary Spanish American literature *(Siglo Veinte,* 1968).

TWAYNE'S WORLD AUTHORS SERIES

A Survey of the World's Literature

Sylvia E. Bowman, Indiana University

GENERAL EDITOR

MEXICO

John P. Dyson, Indiana University

EDITOR

Mariano Azuela

(*TWAS 119*)

TWAYNE'S WORLD AUTHORS SERIES (TWAS)

The purpose of TWAS is to survey the major writers—novelists, dramatists, historians, poets, philosophers, and critics—of the nations of the world. Among the national literatures covered are those of Australia, Canada, China, Eastern Europe, France, Germany, Greece, Italy, Japan, Latin America, New Zealand, Poland, Russia, Scandinavia, Spain, and the African nations, as well as Hebrew, Yiddish, and Latin Classical literature. This survey is complemented by Twayne's United States Authors Series and English Authors Series.

The intent of each volume in these series is to present a critical-analytical study of the works of the writer; to include biographical and historical material that may be necessary for understanding, appreciation, and critical appraisal of the writer; to present all material in clear, concise English— but not to vitiate the scholarly content of the work by doing so.

Mariano Azuela

By LUIS LEAL

University of Illinois

MARIANO AZUELA

To My Wife

.

Preface

MARIANO AZUELA is probably Mexico's best known novelist, both inside and outside his country. To what circumstances can this popularity be attributed? The fact that his novels are associated with the first major revolution of the twentieth century may perhaps explain it. Had he stopped writing novels when the Mexican Revolution began in 1910, he would today be considered by literary critics as just one more of the many novelists who during the last decades of the last century and the first of the present one wrote Naturalistic novels in imitation of those of Zola. He would be placed below such novelists as Federico Gamboa, and even perhaps José López Portillo y Rojas. But Azuela, although a contemporary of the Naturalists, rose to the challenge and identified himself with the twentieth century by joining Madero and his revolutionary movement against the past. He became one of the most important chroniclers of that earth-shaking upheaval which preceded the Russian revolution by seven years.

Azuela's novels of the Mexican Revolution, especially *Los de abajo* (*The Underdogs*), have withstood the test of time and are still read and commented upon. *Los de abajo* has been translated into the major languages of the world, has gone through many editions in the Spanish-speaking world, and remains today one of Mexico's best-known novels.

Azuela's works, indeed, are the best records of Mexico's social change, of the transition from the past to the present, of the abandonment of methods, techniques, and institutions reminiscent of the colonial period, and of the adoption of new ways of life and the creation of new social institutions. In his early novels Azuela depicted a world ruled by tyrannical *hacendados* (feudal lords) and a way of life reminiscent of that prevailing during the Middle Ages. Writing under the dictatorial regime of Porfirio Díaz, master of Mexico for thirty years, Azuela was both perceptive enough to see the evils of the society in which he lived and brave enough to publish his novels criticizing that society. The fact that he was not punished, as was his contemporary Heriberto Frías, indicates that the regime did not consider him dangerous enough to be silenced or that his novels had not attained the necessary publicity. Azuela was not then writing in Mexico City, but in his native Lagos de Moreno in the State of Jalisco. He was at that time an unknown country doctor who wrote novels to relieve boredom. But there is no ambiguity in the powerful denunciation of the rotten social system that prevailed under Díaz, and which Azuela dared to expose in such novels as *Mala yerba (Marcela)*.

When the revolution began in 1910, Azuela immediately sided with Madero and accepted his program, which he tried to make known in his native state. At the same time, he began to write about the upheaval. In his first novel of the revolution, published in 1911 under the title *Andrés Pérez, maderista [maderista:* follower of Madero], the author expressed the fear of a betrayal of the movement by the reactionary forces which had just been displaced but had managed to keep power in their hands. His fear was not in vain, for two years later Madero was assassinated and Victoriano Huerta and the counterrevolutionaries, among them Díaz' nephew, assumed power. Azuela, in 1913, joined Pancho Villa's forces, with the purpose of fighting to preserve Madero's ideals and of preventing a return to the past. His experiences as an army doctor are well depicted in *Los de abajo,* the best novel of the revolution.

In spite of the fact that he had published that novel, he remained unrecognized until 1924, when a debate about the nature of Mexican literature led some critics to his discovery. This event coincided with the interest in the revolution created by the painters Diego Rivera and José Clemente Orozco, who had been commissioned by the government to do a series of murals on public buildings depicting the struggle for freedom. Azuela had previously done the same in his novels, achieving the same esthetic effect. From here on, his future was assured.

Azuela's life has been investigated by several biographers, although not always with accuracy. He himself was interested in leaving for posterity some information about his life and works, although fragmentary, and at times even chaotic. From his own writings, published in three volumes by the Fondo de Cultura Económica in Mexico City, as well as from other sources, an attempt has been made to present here a short but coherent biography, to serve as an introduction to the study of his novels.

Since Azuela is famous as a novelist and not as a doctor, emphasis has been given to the study of his fiction. All his novels and short stories have been examined, in chronological order, from the point of view of contents and technique. Less emphasis has been given to his biographies, his theater, and his nonfiction. They have been included to present a complete picture of Azuela's writings.

The novels, which form the bulk of his writings, have been classified into five groups: the early novels, the novels of the revolution, the experimental novels, the political novels, and the posthumous novels. Each one has been studied as a complete whole. In a concluding chapter, however, an analysis has been made of Azuela's craft of fiction, as found throughout his works. Here the same novels have been studied from the point of view of technique, subject matter, theme, characterization, and style. The purpose of this chapter is to trace common characteristics as well as to present Azuela's fiction as a whole.

Mariano Azuela wrote with a purpose. His medical training and his patients led him to see life through the eyes of a doctor. All his energies were dedicated to the improvement of Mexico's physical and spiritual health. Since he could be more effective as a novelist than he could as a politician, he chose the novel as his tool. These novels could therefore be interpreted not only as exposés of Mexico's illnesses, but also as prescriptions for a better future. Azuela the novelist could not forget Azuela the doctor. Medicine and fiction were his two great loves, neither of which he could give up until his death.

LUIS LEAL

Urbana, Illinois

Acknowledgments

I WOULD like to acknowledge my thanks to Mr. Enrique Azuela for the information he so kindly gave me, and for allowing me to quote from the works of his father, as published in three volumes by the Fondo de Cultura Económica of Mexico City; to Dr. Pedro Frank de Andrea of Editorial Studium of Mexico City for permitting me to use materials from my book *Mariano Azuela, vida y obra;* to the Department of Spanish, Italian, and Portuguese of the University of Illinois for the financial assistance in the copying of the manuscript; to Mr. Guillermo Rojas, Mr. Robert Carter, and Mrs. Bettie Baer for their assistance in putting the manuscript in final form; to Professor John P. Dyson of Indiana University for his careful reading of the manuscript and his useful suggestions; and to my wife, without whose help and encouragement this book would never have been written.

Contents

Chronology

1873   Mariano Azuela born in Lagos de Moreno, Jalisco, Mexico, January 1; first child of Evaristo Azuela and Paulina González.

1887   Continues his studies in Guadalajara, Jalisco.

1892   Begins study of medicine at University of Guadalajara.

1896   Publishes first story, "Impresiones de un estudiante."

1899   Receives medical degree August 18. Begins practice in Lagos de Moreno.

1900   Marries school sweetheart, Carmen Rivera, on September 14.

1902   Birth of first son, Salvador, today Director of publishing house Fondo de Cultura Económica.

1903   Azuela wins prize in local literary contest with short story "De mi tierra." First short trip to Mexico City.

1904   Helps edit the literary review *Kalendas.*

1907   Publishes first novel, *María Luisa,* written earlier.

1908   Publishes *Los fracasados,* novel written in 1906.

1909   Publishes third novel, *Mala yerba.*

1910   With the help of friends, among them José Becerra, forms in Lagos a political committee to help Madero.

1911   After Madero's revolutionary triumph, Azuela is named political leader of Lagos, a position he held from May until July. Publishes *Andrés Pérez, maderista.*

1912   *Sin amor,* novel written earlier.

1913   Madero assassinated. Azuela joins the revolution against Victoriano Huerta.

1914   Writes *Los caciques.* Azuela joins Villa, serving as doctor in the army of General Julián Medina. In December he is appointed state's Director of Public Instruction. Begins to write *Los de abajo.*

1915 Villa defeated by Obregón in Celaya, April 16. Azuela takes refuge in El Paso, Texas, where he had arrived in October. His novel *Los de abajo* appears in installments in the newspaper *El Paso del Norte,* from October to December.
1916 Return of Azuela to Mexico City. Withdraws from politics.
1917 Publishes *Los caciques.*
1918 Publishes the novel *Las tribulaciones de una familia decente,* the novelettes *Las moscas* and *Domitilo quiere ser diputado,* and the short story "De como al fin lloró Juan Pablo," all of them about the revolution.
1922 Begins to work in Consultorio III, a public clinic.
1923 Publishes the experimental novel *La Malhora.*
1924– Mexican critics "discover" *Los de abajo.* Azuela attains
1925 recognition as a novelist. Publishes his second experimental novel, *El desquite.*
1927 Third and last experimental novel, *La luciérnaga.*
1928 Writes, but does not publish for political reasons, the novel *El camarada Pantoja.* The French translation of *Los de abajo* begins to appear in *Le Monde.*
1929 *The Underdogs,* first English translation of *Los de abajo.*
1930 *Ceux de'en bas,* second French translation of *Los de abajo. Die Rotte,* first German translation of *Los de abajo.*
1932 *Marcela: A Mexican Love Story,* American translation of *Mala yerba,* by Anita Brenner.
1933– Biographical novel *Pedro Moreno, el insurgente* appears
1934 in the newspaper *El Nacional,* Mexico City.
1935 Publishes *Los precursores,* a collection of three stories.
1937 Decides to publish *El camarada Pantoja.*
1938 Publishes *San Gabriel de Valdivias, comunidad indígena.*
1939 *Regina Landa,* novel critical of bureaucrats in Mexico.
1940 *Avanzada,* novel critical of new labor bosses. *Los de abajo* and *Mala yerba* made into movies.
1941 *Nueva burguesía,* novel critical of the new rich.
1942 Becomes a member of the Seminario de Cultura Mexicana. Publishes the biography *El padre Agustín Rivera.*
1943 April 8, Azuela is named, by President Manuel Avila Camacho, a life member of the Colegio Nacional.
1944 *La marchanta,* novel about life in Mexico City.
1946 *La mujer domada.*

1947   *Cien años de novela mexicana,* literary criticism. *La marchanta* made into a movie. Finishes *Esa sangre.*
1949   *Sendas perdidas.* Receives the Premio Nacional de Artes y Ciencias. Retires from his position as a doctor in the Department of Health and Public Assistance.
1951   *Pedro Moreno, el insurgente* dramatized.
1952   March 1, Azuela dies of a heart attack. Buried in the Rotonda de Hombres Ilustres in Mexico City.
1955   *La maldición* published by the Fondo de Cultura Económica.
1956   *Esa sangre* published by the Fondo.
1958   *Obras completas,* volumes I and II.
1960   *Obras completas,* volume III.
1968   *Tres novelas de Mariano Azuela* (contains *La Malhora, El desquite* and *La luciérnaga*).

CHAPTER 1

Champion of the Underdogs

ALTHOUGH Mexico had obtained its political independence in
1821, by the middle of the century its social organization was
not unlike that which had prevailed during the colonial period. The
only difference seemed to be that now the rulers were ruthless
generals instead of decadent noblemen. Real power was still concentrated in the hands of the military, the clergy, and the upper
classes. This state of affairs came to a head in 1855, the year when
Santa Anna, who had misgoverned the nation for two decades, was
forced to resign and leave the country. General Juan Alvarez, one
of Santa Anna's opponents, was elected president the same year.
During his administration, Benito Juárez, famous for his integrity
and for his outstanding performance as governor of the State of
Oaxaca, and who held the position of Minister of Justice, drafted
the first law of reform, limiting the powers of the military and
ecclesiastical courts. The reaction of the conservatives was immediate, and Alvarez was forced to resign in favor of Ignacio Comonfort. The latter called a constituent assembly, and a new Constitution
was adopted in 1857. This document was the first effort in Latin
America to liberate the common people from the colonial system of
dominance by the privileged classes. It abolished titles of nobility,
established the supremacy of the state over the church, and granted
religious freedom and freedom of speech.

The conservatives were strongly opposed to the new Constitution
and forced Comonfort to resign. The same year Juárez, who was
President of the Supreme Court of Justice, became President of
Mexico. The result was the "Three Year War" or "War of Reform." The conservative forces were, however, unable to regain
power. Juárez, who had been recognized by the government of the
United States, was re-elected in 1861. The conservatives did not
give up. With the help of Napoleon III, who saw the opportunity
of extending his empire to Mexico, they were able to defeat

Juárez. Napoleon sent to Mexico the ill-fated Maximilian of Austria, whose tragic reign lasted three short years. Upon his return to power and re-election in 1867, Juárez tried to implement the Constitution and to reorganize the nation. His untimely death in 1872 put an end to his experiment in reform. The new president, Sebastián Lerdo de Tejada, tried to continue Juárez' policies but met with strong resistance from the conservatives, now reorganized under the leadership of a young and popular general. This new rising star, Porfirio Díaz, was to become the new master of Mexico. He ignored the Constitution and ruled the country with an iron hand from 1876 until he was forced to resign in 1911. Under his administration—he was systematically re-elected every four years—the nation entered a period of forced peace and false prosperity. Under a thin cover of material progress, the country was to sink to new lows of ignorance, injustice, and suppression of political and individual rights. Díaz allowed the upper classes to regain all their privileges, while most of the population lived in poverty. The *peones,* who had never fared very well, now found themselves living under conditions unknown since the colonial period. Into this world Mariano Azuela, the future champion of the underdogs, was to be born.

I *The Formative Years*

In the year following Juárez' death, two men that were to be prominent in the history of contemporary Mexico were born not far from each other. In San Pedro de las Colonias, in the northern state of Coahuila, Francisco I. Madero, the future revolutionary leader, was born on October 30, 1873. The first day of the same year a child had been born to a storekeeper in the town of Lagos de Moreno, in the west central state of Jalisco. Mariano Azuela's parents, Evaristo Azuela and Paulina González, unlike Madero's well-to-do parents, were members of the middle class. Don Evaristo had to borrow a few hundred pesos from a "rich" brother to establish himself as an independent grocer in Lagos de Moreno. He did so well in his store that after a year he was able to save enough to pay his debt and buy a piece of land in town, where he later built his own store. It was in this environment that the future novelist grew up, and it was from his father's store that he saw, as a boy, the first unsuccessful uprising against the Díaz government.

Mariano's father had a small farm not far from town where the boy spent his summer vacations. It was there that he learned the typical speech of the farmers and ranchers of Jalisco, which he was later to reproduce faithfully in his novels. At the ranch he learned more, he tells us, than he did at the elementary school he attended; or at the Liceo de Varones of Father Guerra, where he studied Latin, grammar, and physics; or from the town's priest, who voluntarily supplemented the meager curriculum of the Liceo with private preparatory tutoring.

Azuela's interest in literature, and especially in novels, was of early origin. While still in elementary school, he began to read Dumas. "Inside the soap boxes," he recollected, "my father used to hide some prohibited books, among them some novels like *The Count of Monte Cristo.* . . . When my father dozed in his easy chair, I used to sneak to the attic and here enjoy the forbidden book." [1] When he told a friend at school what he was reading, the latter's comment was most astonishing: "Alexander Dumas! . . . My father says that it is a sin to read his books." [2] These were the great adventures of his early years. But this peaceful life was to end soon, as he had to leave home and go alone to Guadalajara to continue his studies.

II *In Guadalajara: The Medical Student*

In 1887, at the age of fourteen, Mariano Azuela said good-bye to his parents, his friends, and his beloved ranch and went to Guadalajara to continue his studies at the seminary, fulfilling the wishes of his mother. His first year in Guadalajara was not a happy one. As soon as he completed a course in ethics and religion he left the seminary, regaining his liberty. "The priesthood," he confessed, "never attracted me, and my passage through this institution was incidental." [3] After leaving the seminary in 1889, he registered in the Liceo de Varones del Estado, then located in the building which now houses the State Museum in downtown Guadalajara. Upon transferring from the seminary to the Liceo, which was a public institution, he had to find a place to stay. Following his father's advice, he went to live in the boarding house of Dr. Alvarado, not far from the seminary and where some students from that institution were staying. Life in Dr. Alvarado's home was not much different from that at the seminary. "In the boarding house," Azuela tells us, "the atmosphere of the Seminary predominated, since most of the boarders were seminarists, students of theology. The strictest discipline was observed: at dawn every one had to be on his feet in order to attend mass at Santa Mónica (again the Seminary); at six, breakfast consisting of a glass of milk and scant bread; then, some would go to school, and others, to their rooms to study." [4] At one o'clock sharp, a meager lunch was served, after which the seminarists, well comforted, would discuss the morning lectures. The lord of the mansion, Don Gumersindo, as well as some of the boarders, appear in Azuela's early novelette, *María Luisa.* That this excellent description of life in a boarding house was taken from reality is verified when Azuela, in his sketchy autobiography, *El novelista y su ambiente,*[5] repeats almost word for word the same description.[6]

It was in this same year, 1889, that Azuela wrote what can be considered his first prose. These early notes about life in Guadalajara, in which descriptions of women predominate, were collected with other sketches (written beween that year and 1897), under the title *Registro.*[7] Although of no importance from a literary point of view, they relate experiences which no doubt left an impression on the character of the future novelist.

Life at Dr. Alvarado's boarding house was too tame for a young man no longer interested in the priesthood, and therefore Azuela moved before the year was over to a new boarding house on Belén Street, where he was freer to come and go as he pleased. It was during this year (1890), his second at the Liceo de Varones, that Azuela really began to live and to know Guadalajara. His literary experiences were also broadened. He discovered other novelists, among them Galdós; Isaacs, the famous author of *María;* Lesage; and Gautier. He spent summer vacations at his father's ranch near Guadalajara. He no doubt was attraced to the province by the presence there of his school sweetheart, Carmen Rivera, the niece of the famous philosopher of Lagos, Doctor Agustín Rivera. During these visits to the ranch, Mariano would pass the time preparing adaptations of French romantic dramas. One night he staged *El conde Rouffet de Borbón.* Doña Carmen remembers that when this particular play was presented, in which Mariano was director and actor, the public, made up mostly of local farmers, would go to sleep soon after the curtain was raised. "But the moment would come when they all suddenly woke up. It was when, according to the script, firecrackers would explode on the stage.

Mariano felt happy then, as the noise gave him back his audience for at least fifteen minutes more." [8] This interest in the theater was to remain with him throughout his life.

In 1891 Azuela finished his preparatory school and the following year registered in the School of Medicine at the University of Gaudalajara, where he was to spend the next eight years. In 1899 he received his medical degree. The two years prior to this, he held a position as statistical assistant in the Civil Hospital of Guadalajara, and in 1899 he was even active in the Fifth Police District, helping with problems related to medicine.

The study of medicine did not absorb all of Azuela's attention. In fact, he devoted a great deal of time to the reading of novels, the form of literature that most attracted him. His great discovery was Balzac. It was customary among medical students in Guadalajara, Azuela tells us, to exchange the books they had aready read. In one of those exchanges he received three novels by Balzac, a writer then unknown to him; the novels were *Ursule Mirouet, La cousine Bette,* and *Heroine.* The experience of reading Balzac he could never forget, such was the impression that the French novelist made upon him:

It was during a hot June afternoon when, in order to practice my French, I opened one of the three volumes and went out to the small balcony of my room in Belén Street to read it. . . . I read one, two, three pages without noticing it. It became dark, I lit a lamp, and kept on reading until midnight. With much surprise I realized then that I had forgotten to eat supper.[9]

Other students of medicine, who did not live in the same boarding house but who visited frequently, introduced him to other Realists of the French school: Maupassant, Flaubert, Daudet, and the brothers Goncourt. "It was the realist school," he wrote, "which definitely conquered me and left in my imagination and my way of thinking a profound and indelible mark." [10] If the Realists had fascinated him from the beginning, the Naturalists at first repelled him, but they too were to captivate him with their technique:

One Sunday morning—I remember clearly that moment in my student days—reading *La Linterna de Diógenas,* a Catholic weekly published in Guadalajara, I came across an exceedingly virulent article about the works of a novelist unknown to me: Emile Zola. As usually happens, the diatribe, instead of making me reject the author attacked, awakened in me a strong desire to become acquainted with some of his books. I went to the Public Library and asked for the first book under his name in the catalogue. It turned out to be *The Human Beast.* . . . I could hardly finish reading the first chapter. I closed the book with indignation, disgust, and even anger, and returned it, promising myself that I would not read another line written by this author. But I do not know what happened. The following day I returned to the Library and continued reading until I finished the novel. Emile Zola attracted me with an irresistible force, although his literature, which disconcerted me because of its novelty, made me feel not only a profound aversion for its author, but even physical suffering. Disagreeable, odious, yes, but domineering like a boa constrictor. He had conquered me without my realizing it.[11]

Azuela's interest in reading novels was not merely to pass the time or to break the arduous routine of medical school. He wanted to write them himself. In fact, he was still a medical student when he published his first work. In 1896 he wrote, under the appropriate title "Impresiones de un estudiante," a series of stories which were accepted for publication by a magazine in Mexico City. He did not dare use his own name and signed it with the pseudonym "Beleño." Azuela used one of these "Impressions," which tells the story of a young prostitute who had died in the hospital where he was an intern, two years later to write his first novel. Although the theme is reminiscent of Zola, the descriptions of student life are very much like those found in the French novel *Sor Filomena,* by the Goncourt brothers.

Azuela left medical school in Guadalajara in 1899 with his sheepskin under his arm, ready to practice his profession. By that time he had undoubtedly made up his mind to become a novelist.

III *The Apprentice Years: Doctor or Novelist?*

When Azuela arrived in his home town everything seemed different to him. Although things had not changed, he saw them with different eyes. His attitude toward people, especially, had changed radically. "My absence of twelve years, interrupted now and then by a vacation which I spent at our ranch, had separated me completely from the people whom I thought I knew so well." [12] At least one person, in his opinion, had not changed. On September 12,

1900 he married his boyhood sweetheart, Carmen Rivera, with whom he was to spend the rest of his days. Five sons and five daughters were born to them. Salvador, the oldest, born in 1902, is today active in educational and intellectual circles of Mexico City. Mariano, Jr., born in 1904, has become famous as a lawyer. None of the sons or daughters, however, has followed in his father's footsteps, either in medicine or in the art of the novel.

Azuela's early years as a doctor in his home town of Lagos were not easy. As a general practitioner he had to attend patients suffering from the most varied ailments. For this reason he had to spend his free hours reading medical books and learning what he had not been taught in medical school. In addition, he had to take care of the drug store which he had established for his patients. As a doctor, and indeed in all his activities, Azuela always behaved honorably and with the highest integrity. This was coupled with a great zeal for personal liberty and independence, both of thought and action, which he carried to the point of sacrificing his material well-being. At the same time, he had made up his mind not to participate in local politics.

Nor did Azuela abandon his literary interest and efforts during these years. Fortunately, he found in Lagos a group of intellectuals with whom he became associated. Among the most prominent men of letters belonging to this group, which has been called "The Generation of 1903," [13] were the poet Francisco González León, the lawyers Antonio Moreno y Oviedo and José Becerra, the doctor Bernardo Reina, and Lauro Gallardo. The group would meet monthly with other writers and men of letters to discuss the latest books and to read to each other the poems, stories, or essays that they themselves had composed. It was here that Azuela read chapters of his first novel *María Luisa,* written in Guadalajara where he had served as an intern in the hospital San Miguel de Belén. The group published three volumes of *Ocios literarios* (1905, 1907, 1909) a publication wherein they had collected the best writings of those years. Some time later (1920), four of the members met in Mexico City and published a fourth volume. It is in these anthologies that some of Azuela's earliest stories, sketches, and chapters of future novels appear.

In 1903 the future novelist of the revolution made a journey to Mexico City where he attended concerts, visited art museums, and became acquainted with some of the writers. It was during this time that he began to write short stories of social protest. "Víctimas de la opulencia" and "En derrota" are of interest because they are the first in which Azuela demonstrates that he was aware of the social and economic problems of the country.

From the writing of short stories he went on to write full-length novels. The years 1905 and 1906, years during which he did not publish any work, were dedicated to the writing of *Los fracasados* (*The Failures*), a novel in which he captures vividly the daily life of the city of Lagos as it was during that time. The publication of this novel in 1908 marks the end of the amateur narrator. The period of apprenticeship had ended. From here on he was to devote himself completely to the task of writing novels. *Los fracasados* was to be the first of more than twenty novels written between 1906 and 1949.

Once Azuela had made up his mind to become a novelist, he went to work with great enthusiasm. His next novel, *Mala yerba*,[14] shows a great improvement over *Los fracasados*. Azuela was rapidly learning the art of writing novels. However, he was still under the influence of the Naturalists, especially Zola, whom he admired.

IV *The Coming of the Revolution*

The year 1910 is decisive in the history of Mexico. In that year Francisco I. Madero, born, like Azuela, in 1873, overthrew the government of Porfirio Díaz. In Lagos de Moreno Azuela and his friends sided with Madero and deposed the local politicians. When the revolution triumphed in May, 1911, Azuela was named "Jefe Político" (political boss) of the city of Lagos. But the *caciques* were not to be overthrown so easily. They immediately joined the winning side and became, overnight, *maderistas*. When Azuela appeared at City Hall to take over the government he found the pseudo-*maderistas* there already. It was necessary to make use of force to take possession of his office.

He did not, however, last very long in this position. Hardly two months had gone by when he had to give it up. General elections had not been called yet when the provisional government of Francisco León de la Barra was already conspiring to undermine the revolution. A follower of Díaz was able to take possession of the governorship of Azuela's state, Jalisco. This Azuela could not bear, and he immediately resigned his position. "As if to mock the

Revolution," Azuela bitterly complained, "I had to transfer the office to the same person from whom I had received it." [15]

This experience was decisive in determining the ideology of Azuela. The idea that the revolution had been subverted, an idea that is one of the constants in Azuela's thinking and which appears as underlining the attitude of the author in many of his novels, was born out of this short journey into the field of politics in his home town. "From that moment on," he wrote, "I stopped being the serene observer which I had tried to be in my first four novels. Either as a witness or as an actor in the events that served as basis for my novels I had to be, and in fact was, a partisan and passionate narrator." [16] The first of the novels in which Azuela reflects his new way of thinking is *Andrés Pérez, maderista*, published in Mexico City in 1911 and considered the first novel of the revolution. In it he faithfully depicts the events which took place in his home town when, according to Azuela, the revolution was betrayed.

V *With the Underdogs*

Azuela's accurate appraisal of the political situation was soon to be verified by national events. In 1913 there was a counterrevolution led by Victoriano Huerta. Madero, who had been elected president in 1911, was assassinated by Huerta's followers on February 22, 1913. Huerta assumed the presidency, but was not recognized by some of the governors, nor by President Woodrow Wilson. Madero's followers immediately organized themselves in the north under the leadership of Venustiano Carranza, Alvaro Obregón, and Francisco Villa, and in the south under Emiliano Zapata. In June, 1914, Villa took over the important town of Zacatecas in central Mexico. That same month Mariano Azuela was finishing his novel *Los caciques*. "I was," he said, "touching up the last chapter when groups of Federal soldiers began to arrive. They had been defeated by Villa in Zacatecas. The Revolution had triumphed!" [17]

Huerta's government fell in July, 1914. Unfortunately, a rivalry erupted between Carranza and Obregón on the one side and Villa on the other. In August Carranza entered Mexico City and assumed the title of Primer Jefe. Villa, of course, did not recognize Carranza and decided to fight to the end. Some intellectuals, in order to avoid this unnecessary struggle among revolutionaries, called for a convention at Aguascalientes. Carranza's government was not recognized and, as a result, the administration in Mexico City changed hands. Carranza withdrew to Puebla, and Villa and Zapata took over the capital. Azuela sympathized with the *villistas:* "I found myself," Azuela confessed, "on the side of the party of the Convention of Aguascalientes, not only because I sympathized with its cause, but also because, for me, it represented the legal aspect of the Revolution; in the second place, having decided to side with this party and therefore relinquishing some of my personal liberty by so doing, I found myself on the side of Villa and his followers." [18] This decision to stay with Villa and the *villistas* was to be of the utmost importance in Azuela's life. And it is essential to know this fact in order to understand his attitude toward the Revolution and to interpret his novels.

Azuela's decision to join Villa was not entirely his own. His friend José Becerra, who had already joined Villa's army, was instrumental in making Azuela take sides in the struggle between the two revolutionary factions. Becerra, while serving as attorney in the town of Tequila in the state of Jalisco, had joined the rebel army of General Julián Medina. "When Medina went through Lagos, after the Aguascalientes Convention," Azuela remembered, "he invited me to collaborate in the formation of a government to substitute that of General Manuel M. Diéguez, who was a close friend of Carranza and whose government was unconstitutional". [19] Toward the end of October, 1914, Azuela became a member of General Julián Medina's staff. Medina was then at the city of Irapuato, waiting for the rest of Villa's army, which had left Mexico City after having sided with the provisional government of Eulalio Gutiérrez, who was named acting president of Mexico by the convention. Azuela was appointed head of the medical staff of General Medina's army, with the rank of Lieutenant Colonel. While in Irapuato with Medina, Azuela conceived the idea of writing *Los de abajo* (*The Underdogs*), his most famous novel. Medina, according to Azuela, was fond of telling him his adventures as a revolutionary general, many of which Azuela elaborated and adopted for his novel, of which Medina was to be the hero.

Pursued by Carranza, Medina had to withdraw with his army toward Guadalajara, where he arrived in December, 1914. There Azuela was named Director of Public Education by the governor of the state, a position he held less than a month. Medina and his followers had been forced to abandon Guadalajara and withdraw into the mountains. During this short stay in Guadalajara, Azuela had continued writing his novel. It was here that he decided to name the hero Demetrio Macías. At the same time, he gave up the idea of elaborating upon the portrayal of Medina in order to give the hero traits peculiar to other officers he had met.

Villa's defeat by General Obregón at the city of Celaya April 16, 1915, forced Medina to move his army to Lagos de Moreno, where he remained until May. But there was no let-up. They were pursued by Obregón's army until they were forced to withdraw to the north. Azuela, meanwhile, had been separated from the main body of the troops. He had remained in the town of Tepatitlán (near Guadalajara) to take care of some wounded soldiers. It was here that he became acquainted with a young colonel, Manuel Caloca, who had been wounded in the battle that took place in Tlaquepaque, just outside Guadalajara. As the *carrancistas* were threatening to take the town, Azuela, Caloca, and eighty of their men left Tepatitlán and took refuge in the mountains of Juchipila. There they were overtaken by a group of federal soldiers. "With Caloca on a stretcher," Azuela relates, "we were ambushed by a group of *carrancistas* at the bottom of a canyon. But Caloca's men were excellent horsemen, among whom were many mountaineers, and they easily were able to get out of the trap and defeat the enemy. I, meanwhile, in a cave on the side of the mountain, was taking notes for the final scene of the novel." [20]

Although the *villistas* won a few skirmishes, their defeat at Celaya had sealed their fate. Villa's troops had to withdraw all the way to the border. Caloca's group, after going through the small town of Limón, reached Aguascalientes, where Azuela took Caloca to the hospital and was able to operate on him there and restore his health. They both took the train to the north toward Chihuahua. In the city of Chihuahua, Caloca stayed in the hospital and Azuela continued north toward El Paso, Texas. There, later, Caloca and Azuela were reunited. Azuela had reached El Paso in October, 1915, with his novel two-thirds completed. In El Paso, away from the smoke of the battlefield, he was able to complete the novel and publish it in the newspaper *El Paso del Norte* between November and December of that same year. "One night in November of 1915," Azuela tells us, "in a hotel room, I was reading a chapter of my novel to a group of expatriates like myself. Among them were Enrique Pérez Arce, Abelardo Medina, Enrique Luna Román, and other professional men, most of them lawyers. When I came to the passage where Demetrio Macías is being carried on a stretcher through the canyon of Juchipila, Manuel Caloca, who was among those who were listening, recognized himself." [21]

It was Enrique Luna Román who first put Azuela in contact with the editor of the newspaper *El Paso del Norte,* a man by the name of Gamiochipi. Before giving his manuscript to Gamiochipi, however, Azuela visited several agents of publishing houses with the purpose of publishing the novel. But they all wanted to send the manuscript to Mexico City, a risky and dilatory business owing to the conditions prevailing during the time. Therefore, Azuela decided to give the novel to Gamiochipi, to be published in the newspaper. As sole payment, Azuela was offered a thousand copies of the book and a loan of three dollars a week while the novel was being published. During the first month after publication, Azuela was able to sell five copies of the book. Today, this first edition has become very rare, and only a few copies are known to exist.

Unhappy in El Paso because of the long separation from his family, Azuela decided to return to Mexico. Early in 1916, taking advantage of the confusion caused by the taking of Ciudad Juárez by the *carrancistas,* Azuela crossed the border and returned to Mexico City by train.

VI *Life in Mexico City*

Mexico City in 1916 was not a pleasant place in which to live. However, Azuela decided to settle with his family in the capital, to withdraw completely from politics, and to dedicate himself to the practice of medicine and to the writing of novels. The first months were not easy. He was penniless. In order to acquire needed funds, he decided to offer his novel *Los caciques* to the newspaper *El Universal.* The novel was accepted for publication by the director of the daily, Félix F. Palavicini, in spite of the fact that the editorial committee had given an adverse report. Azuela remembers, 'Palavicini . . . gave me an order to collect a hundred pesos from the cashier, the value which he had assigned to my book. I left the offices of *El Universal* running, went to Crespo's store and bought a suit and returned home ready to begin practicing my profession." [22]

Azuela began treating patients in the corner drugstore. He became a good friend of the druggists, who sent him all those who asked for medical advice. Soon Azuela saw himself working more than he wanted to. As a result of a typhus epidemic his services were much in demand, as were those of all other doctors in Mexico City. Soon after this Azuela was able to open his own office, located in one of the city's poorest neighborhoods, Peralvillo. "Poor were the patients I had attended in my native state, and poor were my clients in Mexico City," Azuela remarks with pride.[23]

Although his professional work kept him extremely busy, he did not give up writing novels. During these first years in Mexico City he wrote his novels *Las moscas* (*The Flies*),[24] *Domitilo quiere ser diputado* (*Domitilo Wants to Be a Congressman*), *Las tribulaciones de una familia decente* (*The Trials of a Respectable Family*), and a short story, "De como al fin lloró Juan Pablo" ("How Juan Pablo Finally Cried").

In spite of having published all these novels, Azuela in 1919 was still unknown. Perhaps because of this lack of public interest in his writings he became disillusioned and did not publish anything—except two short stories—between 1919 and 1922. He did not give up all hope, however, and decided to try once more. This is the way he felt about the matter: "Around 1921 and 1922, tired of being ignored in spite of the fact that I had published *Los de abajo, Mala yerba,* and *Las tribulaciones de una familia decente,* novels which are now well known, I decided to make a final effort. I made up my mind that if I were to fail again, I would abandon this activity forever."[25]

To arouse the public's attention, or rather that of the critics, Azuela wrote a novel using a new technique. *La Malhora,* a short novel which appeared in 1923, marks a change in Azuela's development as a novelist. He abandoned the theme of the revolution; he abandoned his straightforward style; he abandoned the use of a plot that develops chronologically. Instead, he made a character study of a young girl in Mexico City, describing her life in short, dislocated scenes written in an impressionistic style unlike that of his previous novels. The novel was well received by the critics, but its author still remained an unknown novelist. The book did not sell. This led Azuela to burn all his manuscripts. At this very moment, however, something unusual happened that was to change his life and his future place in Mexican letters.

VII *Recognition at Last*

Toward the end of 1924 the obscure doctor became, from one day to the next, a novelist of national and international fame. What brought about this sudden change? It was, really, the indirect result of a controversy between literary critics who were interested in determining if Mexico had produced a vital literature. Those who defended the existence of such a literature called attention to Azuela's novel, *The Underdogs,* as an example of a work that was not decadent. Among the most important critics taking this position was Professor Francisco Monterde, the discoverer of *Los de abajo.*[26] From this moment on all the newspapers began to print articles about Azuela and to praise his novels. The most popular magazine of the time, *El Universal Ilustrado,* published *Los de abajo* in serial form during January and February of 1925. His friend Gregorio Ortega took the novel to Spain, where two editions appeared in 1927. Two years later Brentano's published the English edition under the title *The Underdogs.*[27] In France two translations appeared almost at the same time. The magazine *Le Monde* serialized the novel, which appeared in its pages between 1928 and 1929 under the title "L'Ouragan."[28] The same translation, published in book form, appeared in 1930 under the title *Ceux de'en bas.* The Preface to this edition, by the famous critic Valéry Larbaud, contributed more than anything else to making Azuela well known in Europe. About the reception that his novel had in France, Azuela had this to say: "I owe to my novel *The Underdogs* one of the sweetest satisfactions that I, as a writer, have received in my life. The famous French novelist and well-known Communist, Henri Barbuse, had my novel translated and published in the magazine *Le Monde,* which he edited. The magazine *Acción Francesa,* a monarchist publication representing the extreme right in France, praised my novel. This is a very significant occurrence for an independent writer and needs no comments."[29] In the same year, 1930, the novel was translated into German and appeared under the title *Die Rotte.* Soon after translations in Japanese, Portuguese, Italian, Russian, and other languages appeared. Azuela had become by now a recognized novelist, a representative of what has come to be known as the novel of the revolution. This sudden recognition had a decided effect on Azuela. He gained confidence in himself and in his work and continued to write and publish novels to the very end. The fact that he became famous with *Los de abajo* and not with the experimental novels made him return to his early style of writing. The cycle that had begun with *La Malhora* (*The Ill-Fated Girl*) in 1925 had ended two years later with *La Luciérnaga* (*The Firefly*). Of this novel, the author had this to say: "My third novel which I wrote[30] using a modern technique is called *La Luciérnaga* and it has been the greatest literary success which I have had in my life, but at the same time it has been the greatest economic failure. Published by Espasa Calpe in Madrid nineteen years ago, only about a thousand copies have been sold, while my other novels have gone through several editions each." [31]

VIII *An Independent Writer*

When Azuela said that the reception of his famous novel in France was a great satisfaction "for an independent writer," he meant ideologically, not economically, independent. However, from 1927 on he became economically independent also. That year he bought his own house at 242 Alamo Street, a street now called Mariano Azuela in his honor. In that house he spent the rest of his life in the company of his family. The house is still in the hands of Azuela's descendants, and don Mariano's study and library has been kept as he left it.

As a family man Azuela was rather strict with his children. The house was divided into two parts, one for the men and the other for the ladies; the five boys lived with the father in the back part of the house; the five girls with the mother in the part of the house nearest the street. This is how doña Carmen Azuela, who still lives in this same house, describes it: "This division was not an absolute reality, as my husband's office, where he attended his patients, was in the front of the house. After he gave up the practice of medicine he had a room built for himself, a kind of workshop, where he remained from five in the morning until late in the afternoon. He always had time, however, to play with his grandchildren and to talk to our sons." [32] He also found relaxation binding his own books and doing some carpentry.

Azuela was a generous and kind man. He cured the poor without charge. He did not even turn away petty thieves who came to see him and who would often steal his hat or his handkerchiefs. But he received his reward by getting from them a knowledge of human nature which helped him to write his novels, in which some of these characters often appéar.

His love of independence kept him from attending parties, social functions, or literary gatherings, but he was interested in the theater, the opera, and the cinema. His love of liberty and his desire to be independent predominated throughout his life and gave direction to his activities. He preferred, as he tells us, to live in abject poverty rather than to submit to the thousand indignities suffered by those who held a government position. As an independent writer he could freely criticize the government and society in general, something he could not do from behind a bureaucratic desk. This independent attitude is reflected in his novels. In those published in 1918 he criticizes Carranza and his method of governing the nation. In *La Luciérnaga* he attacks President Plutarco Elías Calles and his followers. The government is severely criticized in *El camarada Pantoja,* a novel written in 1928 but not published until 1937. Azuela was not fearful of reprisals. He had defied the governments of Díaz, Huerta, Carranza, Calles, and every other politician who was unscrupulous enough to take advantage of his position for personal gain.

But, can a writer constantly attack the government and remain immune? It is true that Azuela was never imprisoned or even admonished. On the contrary, he was offered a position in the Health Department, a position which he accepted, as he said, to pay, with the salary they paid him, the high taxes that the government imposed on his house. "When I was in the Health Department," he wrote, "no one annoyed me. Even more: Don Luis León, who held a high position in Calles' government, encouraged me to publish my works in the government newspaper, *El Nacional,* offering to pay anything I asked for my novels *Los fracasados* and *Pedro Moreno el insurgente.*"[33] And yet, after writing *El camarada Pantoja* Azuela gave up for a few years the writing of novels dealing with contemporary events. He took refuge in Mexican history, leaving behind, as he said, the mudhole into which Mexican politics was sinking.

During this short interlude Azuela produced three semihistorical books: *Pedro Moreno, el insurgente* (1933), *Precursores* (1935), and *El Padre Agustín Rivera* (1942).

Azuela's sojourn into history and biography was short-lived. He soon returned to writing novels. The attraction was irresistible. Even though the political scene may have been a mudhole, he wanted to see if he could do something about it. His novels from that time on are much more critical of the political evils he saw in government and society in general. *Regina Landa* (1939), a novel written at the Health Department, where he studied the inner functioning of the self-perpetuating government bureaucracy, severely criticizes the implications of the political philosophy of President Lázaro Cárdenas. In *San Gabriel de Valdivias* (1938), a novel in which he returns to the rural areas of Mexico for his setting and characters, he has harsh words for the new system imposed by the government upon the formerly independent farmers. He also criticizes those officials who took advantage of the distribution of the land to the peons to enrich themselves and gain political power at the same time. In *Avanzada* (1940) the labor unions and the new labor bosses fall under his critical wrath. And finally in *Nueva burguesía* (finished in 1940, published in 1941), the new, rising middle class in Mexico City is the object of his ridicule and contempt.

IX *The Last Decade*

The last ten years in the life of Azuela were perhaps the least turbulent of his long journey. They were not years of inactivity; on the contrary, it was a period of unremitting literary activity. He published three more novels, literary criticism (on the Mexican novel), and personal memoirs. He left unpublished two more novels and a biography of Francisco I. Madero.

These last ten years were years of triumph for Azuela. He was finally given unreserved recognition and was honored both abroad as well as at home. In May, 1942, Azuela was invited by the Secretary of Education, Octavio Véjar Vázquez, to become a member of the Seminario de Cultura Mexicana. "I accepted the membership in this society with pleasure because," Azuela said with tongue in cheek, "I have run out of bad things to say about our government." [34] In August of the same year he was invited to become a member of the exclusive and traditional Academia Mexicana de la Lengua, an honor reserved for a very limited number of writers. Azuela, showing his independence, did not accept this honor, in spite of the pressure put upon him by family and friends. In the tradition of the great poet Rubén Darío, he could very well have exclaimed: "De las Academias, líbranos, Señor!" (Oh Lord, deliver us from the Academies!).

In April, 1943, Azuela received one of the highest honors that the Mexican government can bestow upon a writer. He was appointed by President Manuel Avila Camacho to take part in the foundation of the new Colegio Nacional and to become one of its twenty members. This unique institution, made up of specialists in the arts and the sciences, was founded with the purpose of creating an educational institute of higher learning whose members were dedicated to research or the creative arts. Among the twenty original members there were, besides the name of Azuela, such prominent persons as the poet Enrique González Martínez, the painter José Clemente Orozco, the critic Alfonso Reyes, the philosopher Samuel Ramos, the novelist Agustín Yañez, the archeologist Alfonso Caso, the physicist Manuel Sandoval Vallarta, the composer Carlos Chávez, and the biologist Isaac Ochoterena. This institute offered no classes and had no students. The only obligation of the members was to give a series of lectures on a subject related to their field of study or special interest.

As in the case of the Academia de la Lengua, Azuela's first reaction upon receiving the invitation to join the Colegio Nacional was to reject it. Friends and members of the family, however, were able this time to prevail upon him to accept the invitation. The same year (1943), he gave a series of lectures on the development of the Mexican novel. He talked about the most important novelists of Mexico during the preceding hundred years, that is, from the publication of the first Mexican novel, *El Periquillo Sarniento* of José Joaquín Fernández de Lizardi, to the appearance of his own novel, *The Underdogs,* in 1916. He did not, however, talk about his own works during this occasion. He discussed the novels of Lizardi, Vicente Riva Palacio, Ignacio M. Altamirano, Rafael Delgado, José López Portillo y Rojas, Emilio Rabasa, Manuel H. San Juan, Federico Gamboa, and Heriberto Frías. These lectures were published in 1947 under the title *Cien años de novela mexicana.*

In the same year, 1943, Azuela received another honor. He was named corresponding member of the Hispanic Society of America. That year was, indeed, crucial for the novelist. An important change took place in his private life. After many years of attending his clients at home, he decided to close his medical office. He continued, nevertheless, to take care of the poor people of the community who came to see him, and his services, as before, were entirely free. At the same time, he continued going to the First Aid Station of the social security program to take care of poor children suffering from minor illnesses. The closing of his office gave Azuela more time to complete unfinished novels. In 1944 he published *La marchanta,* and in 1946 *La mujer domada (The Tamed Woman).* Another novel, *Esa sangre (That Blood),* which is a continuation of one of his early novels, *Marcela (Mala yerba),* was completed in 1947 but left unpublished. His interest in the theater and the cinema, which had always been strong, increased during those last years, especially with the filming of *Los de abajo, Mala yerba,* and *La marchanta.*

The year 1949 was one of the happiest in Azuela's life. Besides publishing his novel *Sendas perdidas (Lost Paths),* the last he published during his lifetime, he received the highest honor the Mexican government can bestow upon an artist: the coveted National Prize in Arts and Sciences. The ceremony took place January 26, 1950, in the residence of the President of Mexico. Miguel Alemán himself gave Azuela the prize. The official speech was delivered by Carlos Chávez, then Director of the National Institute of Fine Arts.

That same year Azuela decided to give up all professional activities and to live on the pension that he was receiving from the Department of Health and the money received from social security. His interest in writing novels diminished, although it is true that in 1949 he put the last touches to his novel *La maldición (The Curse),* the second one that he did not see published. He explained this decreased interest in writing in this way: "During the years that I saw myself forced to retire from all professional activities, I thought that, with the extra time that I had, I would write more than I had been able to do before. But by that time I had lost the desire to do it. And that is why today I divide my time between two activities only, binding books and raising chickens. These are the least offensive activities that I can undertake at my age; except, of course, from the point of view of the books and the chickens." [35]

If his interest in writing novels decreased, it was not so with the theater, for this interest he had sustained since his youth. In 1951,

when his work *Pedro Moreno, el insurgente* was dramatized and
presented under the direction of Víctor Moya, Azuela was very
enthusiastic about the event, praising both the actors and the director during opening night. The director had been interested in
dramatizing the novel *Mala yerba*. But Azuela, remembering the
movie failure, refused to grant permission. Instead, he suggested
that *Pedro Moreno* be presented. Azuela was delighted with the
performance.

After 1949 Azuela wrote his memoirs under the title *Autobiografía del otro* (*The Other Man's Autobiography*), later continued
as *El novelista y su ambiente,* parts I and II. In 1951 his own
state of Jalisco recognized his merit and gave him a gold medal.
At the ceremony another famous writer from Jalisco, the poet
Enrique González Martínez, was present and was also honored.
In spite of his age, Azuela in this same year gave a series of lectures at the summer school of the National University, then directed by Professor Francisco Monterde, a life-long friend of
Azuela.

A month before his death, the novelist suffered his first heart
attack. On February 23, 1952, he suffered the second attack. He
died in his home on March 1 at the age of seventy-nine. The
funeral took place in the Palace of Fine Arts, where his many
friends, as well as the public in general, were able to pay him last
homage. President Miguel Alemán decreed that Azuela be buried
in the Rotunda de Hombres Ilustres, a cemetery dedicated ex-
clusively to Mexico's famous men. The funeral oration was given
by the writer Salvador Novo, at that time director of the drama
department of the Institute of Fine Arts. Also present were Jesús
Silva Herzog, who represented the Colegio Nacional, Luis Garrido,
President of the National University; and the novelist Mauricio
Magdaleno.

Posthumously Azuela has received many honors. In November,
1953, the Colegio Nacional held a ceremony in his honor, at which
time Dr. Antonio Caso pointed out in his speech Azuela's many
merits, both as a writer and as a friend. But perhaps the greatest
tribute paid him has been the publication, by Mexico's outstanding
publishing house, the Fondo de Cultura Económica, of his two
novels, *La maldición* in 1955 and *Esa sangre* in 1956, as well as his
Obras completas in three volumes in 1958 and 1960. The third
volume, prepared by the poet and critic Alí Chumacero, contains

some works that Azuela had never published, such as his biography of Francisco I. Madero.

What was Azuela like? Physically, he was of medium height and well proportioned. He had piercing eyes hidden behind round-rimmed glasses, and his lips were rather thin. His whitish mustache tended to disappear with the passing of the years, and his thick, bushy eyebrows contrasted with his rather thin hair. Morally, Mariano Azuela was completely honest and a lover of truth and fairness, especially of social justice and fair play toward the less fortunate. He was extremely jealous of his independence, and he would rather be alone than compromise his liberty in any way. He was, at the same time, a devoted husband and good father. In his habits, he was methodical. He began to work every day at six in the morning and wrote a certain number of pages daily.

Among his many famous friends were José Vasconcelos, José Clemente Orozco, Enrique González Martínez, and Diego Rivera. In his library there is a book on art presented to him by Diego Rivera in which the painter wrote the following dedication: "To Dr. Mariano Azuela, the only great writer that the Mexican Revolution has produced. With my admiration and profound affection."

Of Azuela it can be said that he had a rebellious spirit, tempered by his great love of humanity and his hope that a more perfect society could be established in the future. For this end he worked with sincerity and great energy all his life.

CHAPTER 2

The Early Writings

I *Azuela's Precursors*

DURING the colonial period the novel in Mexico, unlike poetry, did not flourish. It is true that there were some works that contain narrative elements, such as the *Sirgueros de la Virgen* (*Songs in Praise of the Virgin,* 1620) by Francisco Bramón, a pastoral romance with a slender narrative thread; *Los infortunios de Alonso Ramírez* (1680), a historical narrative structured like a picaresque novel; and *La portentosa vida de la Muerte* (1792) by Joaquín Bolaños, in which personified Death relates her own life. But it was not until 1816 that José Joaquín Fernández de Lizardi wrote what could be called a true novel—*El Periquillo Sarniento.*[1]

Although Lizardi used the picaresque structure which is a Spanish form, the novel depicts Mexican society at the end of the colonial period.[2] Lizardi's thinking was influenced by French writers such as Rousseau, and it clashed with the traditional Spanish attitudes. The most important aspect of the novel, however, is not its philosophy, but the popular elements he introduced into literature, such as the language and the characters.

Unfortunately, Lizardi's example was not followed. The novelists of the Romantic period looked again toward Europe for inspiration and produced second-rate sentimental romances unworthy of the name. The exceptions were those written by Luis G. Inclán and Manuel Payno. Inclán's novel, *Astucia* (1865), gives an excellent picture of rural Mexico. His characters are Mexican rancheros, and his style reproduces the language spoken in central Mexico. Manuel Payno, a contemporary of Inclán, wrote his best novel late in life. His *Bandidos de Río Frío* did not appear until 1889, although his first novel had been published thirty years earlier. In *Los bandidos* one finds again a true picture of Mexico and its people. His characters, some of which are taken from real life, are representatives of Mexican society. Payno, as well as other novelists writing at the time, were following the precepts of Ignacio M. Altamirano, who had recommended that they write about Mexican subjects in a style worthy of a national literature. He himself had written novels and novelettes such as *Clemencia* (1869), *La navidad en las montañas* (1871),[3] and *El Zarco* (1886; first ed., 1901), to mention only the most outstanding.

French Realists and Spanish Regionalists had a powerful influence upon Mexican novelists. During the last three decades of the nineteenth century there was a period of transition between Romanticism and Realism in novelists such as Rafael Delgado, the author of *La Calandria* (1891); José Tomás de Cuéllar, painter of Mexican customs in an ironical vein; and José López Portillo y Rojas, whose Regionalist novel, *La parcela* (1898), is a perfect example of the influence of the Spanish novelists, especially Pereda. Following Altamirano's advice, López Portillo had chosen a Mexican subject and located his novel in his native state of Jalisco, but it turned out to be, as Azuela pointed out, a halfway success, since his characters speak more like Spanish farmers than Mexican peons.

After these novelists of transition come the true Naturalists, among whom Gamboa is the most representative. His novels, such as *Suprema ley* (1896), *Metamorfosis* (1899), *Santa* (1903), and *Reconquista* (1908), written under the influence of Zola and the Naturalists,[4] represent the best effort in fiction that had been attempted up to that time. These novels are well constructed, well written, and well motivated.

Azuela also began writing under the influence of the French Realists. His first four novels, written between 1907 and 1909, still reflect the influence of that school. Speaking about the writing of his first novel, he said: "I was in my fifth year of Medical School [in Guadalajara] immersed, not so much in the study of pathology and therapeutics, as in the reading of the Realistic novels of France and Spain, then at their highest in popularity. The novel *Sor Filomena* by Goncourt had enchanted me with its admirable descriptions of the life of the students of medicine during their internship in the hospitals of Paris. Who of us then did not dream about the Latin Quarter of Paris, as described by so many poets and novelists?"[5] It must be remembered that during that time the works of French novelists, even those of inferior quality, were translated into Spanish and published in every newspaper and

magazine throughout Spain and Latin America. If a Mexican
novelist wanted to sell his books, he had to imitate the French
writers, as the public was used to reading this type of novel. About
this problem Azuela commented: 'I wrote *María Luisa* [his first
novel] fifty-three years ago. At that time the Realistic school was
at its peak. The novelists that predominated were Flaubert, the
Goncourt brothers, Zola, Daudet, and Maupassant, and we students
were as eager to read them as we were to read the Spaniards
Pereda and Valera. The influence of the Romantic writers had not
yet, however, disappeared; most readers still enjoyed the literature
of Victor Hugo, George Sand, and Eugène Sue, very far yet from
the psychological complications that today even the barbers
demand." [6]

Why did Azuela and other Mexican novelists imitate the French
authors? Although the problem is much more complex than it
appears to be, it may be said that during the Díaz administration
writers were trying to adapt themselves to a new official philosophy
and to a new way of life brought about by the break with the past
that had taken place among the intellectuals and the political
leaders during the period of reform under Juárez. Having rejected
the Spanish tradition and unable to go back to an Indian heritage,
they had to turn to France, since writers in other Spanish-speaking
countries had nothing original to offer. The United States, although
geographically close, could not be imitated due to the difference
in language and cultural backgrounds. On the other hand, French
culture could be easily assimilated, as all the educated Mexicans
of the period spoke French. By imitating the French writers, who
were in the forefront of literary development in Europe, Mexican
authors could also demonstrate their intellectual independence from
Spain, which they had not done up to that time. The experiment—
for it was an experiment—was so successful that the result was a
literary reform, especially in style.

As a result of this imitation authors like Manuel Gutiérrez
Nájera were creating a new Spanish style, a style characterized by
a lightness and grace unknown to the traditional Castilian writers.
Gutiérrez Nájera and other Mexican *modernistas* began to write
artistic short stories and novels in which the form, and not the
subject matter, was the most important element. Of one of those
modernistas Azuela had this to say: "Amado Nervo wrote de-
lightful and incomparable novels which reflect his poetic nature as

much as his verse."⁷ Of one of his novels he said: "I like *El Bachiller* of Amado Nervo more than any of the novels of the most famous Mexican novelists."⁸ These two influences, the Mexican *modernistas* and the French Realists, were to be predominant in the formation of Azuela as a novelist.⁹

II *The First Stories*

Azuela began writing simple sketches in 1889, when he was still a medical student in Guadalajara. Unpublished during his life (they appeared for the first time in volume III of his *Obras completas* in 1960), these sketches show Azuela's interest in people and in direct characterization. The first part, called "Registro," is a collection of pictures of girls he knew; the second part, called "Páginas íntimas," is a recording of adolescent adventures.

From the simple sketch Azuela went on to write regular stories. The first that he published were appropriately named "Impresiones de un estudiante." They appeared in the magazine *Gil Blas Cómico* of Mexico City between March 5 and November 22, 1896, signed with the pseudonym "Beleño." The last one is the story of a prostitute who dies in the hospital. One of the students using her corpse to practice an autopsy had been her seducer. The story is important in the study of Azuela as a novelist because the plot was later developed into a full-length novel.

Except for another sketch, "Esbozo," published in *El Noticioso* of Guadalajara on March 27, 1897, under the pseudonym "Fierabrás," Azuela did not publish anything until 1903. The stories which began to appear that year show a definite improvement over the "Impresiones." Azuela has learned to use irony and even sarcasm in the portrayal of character, as can be seen in "Esbozo," a story about a mediocre medical student. He is now conscious of the many social injustices prevalent in Mexico and denounces them in "De mi tierra," a story awarded first prize in a literary contest held in Lagos in 1903. At this early period, however, the social protest was secondary to the telling of the anecdote. Teodora, the servant girl seduced by the master of the house, has to explain to her husband why their son has blond hair.

A theme that is to recur in many of Azuela's works, that of the tragedy of the poor caused by injustices of the rich, is introduced in "Víctimas de la opulencia" (1904); a young servant girl sacrifices

her own son so that the son of the lady of the house may live. The
social protest, however, is weakened by the sentimental ending.

Another story published in 1904, "En derrota," has a rural
setting and deals with the conflict between a peon and the overseer's son, who fight over Camila, a girl very much like the Camila
of *The Underdogs,* and which undoubtedly served as a prototype.
The elements of Naturalism of this and the preceding stories,
even if subdued, already point to the kind of novel that Azuela
will write during this early period.

III   *The First Novel*

The first novel that Azuela published, *María Luisa*[10] (1907),
is based on the last story of the seven which appeared under the
collective title "Impresiones de un estudiante." *María Luisa* is the
story of a seventeen-year-old girl who has been seduced by a
medical student. María Luisa, the protagonist, is the victim of her
own degenerate background, but the author does not dramatize her
life as a prostitute, in the manner of a Nana or even a Santa. It is
obvious that Azuela, at that time, was not interested in describing,
like the French Naturalists, the worst aspects of life. The emphasis
falls, rather, on the protest against society for allowing a young
girl like María Luisa to be perverted by the ideal offspring of the
well-to-do. If Azuela, in this novel, had described life in Guadalajara's houses of ill repute, he would have anticipated Gamboa's
Santa, a novel dealing with prostitution in Mexico City and which
leans heavily on Zola's *Nana.*

María Luisa, which is more like an elaborated short story than
a novel, has serious defects. The characterization of María Luisa
and some of the others is inconsistent and often contradictory.
Pancho, seducer of María Luisa and a "heartless cynic," is sometimes presented as a likable fellow: "He was not," the novelist
says, "in effect a bad fellow; his innocent-looking eyes and the
accent of his perfectly frank speech confirmed the sincerity of his
words." A much more serious defect is the sudden change in the
nature of the characters. Pancho seduces María Luisa without
actually wanting to, and the friendship between the protagonist
and her friend Ester is not clearly drawn, as their mutual feelings
change without apparent reason.

Besides poor characterization and motivation, the plot structure
is rather weak. Immediately after María Luisa begins drinking, the

narrative is cut short. In the next and last chapter, three years later, she is in the hospital on the verge of death, a victim of tuberculosis, alcoholism, and pneumonia, the result of her decadent life. While this is plausible in life, it cannot be accepted in a novel without some of the events that lead to the climax being dramatized, so that the illusion of the passing of time is created.

But if the novel has defects it also has its good points. The dialogues are interesting and never dull; the speech of the characters reflects their regional and social status: it is neither vulgar, nor does it show affectation. At the same time, Azuela does not squirm, as do other Mexican Realists and Naturalists, at the use of the Spanish typical of the nation. Indeed, this is a distinguishing feature of Azuela's style, as are the short, fine descriptions of the Mexican landscape.

In the numerous *costumbrista* sketches, especially those in which he describes the boarding houses patronized by the students, Azuela demonstrates his satirical and sometimes humorous attitude. The emotive scenes, like the fight between María Luisa and the aunt who serves as a go-between, add a dramatic touch. No less interesting is the characterization of El Chato, because here Azuela uses for the first time a technique which he is to develop fully later, that of capturing the essential nature of a person by presenting, and often integrating, both his physical and his moral traits. El Chato has a deformed body and his face, in spite of his youth, is like a parchment. His receding chin shows a reddish tinge, the result of his licentiousness. Morally, he is sly, cunning, and contemptuous. This contemptuous attitude, however, turns out to be nothing but "a flash of malignance in the abyss of his stupidity." [11] The picture of a degenerate student appears frequently in Azuela's novels. He had become well acquainted with the type during his student days in the boarding houses of Guadalajara and could draw El Chato from firsthand observation.

While his first novel is not lacking in literary merits, its primary value lies in what it reveals about the origins of Azuela's narrative art. Here are the beginnings of the making of the future novelist of the revolution. Within these early pages there is a glimmer of the theme of his masterpiece, *The Underdogs:* "María Luisa was the daughter of pure accident. She was born when soldiers of our eternal revolutions came into town stained with the blood of their own brothers, seeking the pleasures of the flesh and unleashing

their powerful instincts. After being satiated with death, they
wanted to be satiated with life." [12]

Azuela himself described his first novelistic work as "an observation of the students in Guadalajara at the end of the nineteenth century," and the protagonist as "a sister of Mimí Pinsón,
of Margarita Gautier, of Musseta; a spurious sister, but nevertheless a sister. A novel of my youth, of my student days in the sweet,
romantic and passionate Guadalajara." [13]

IV Los Fracasados

Los fracasados (*The Failures*), published in 1908, is Azuela's
first full-length novel. Written in Lagos de Moreno in 1906, it did
not appear until two years later.[14] The theme of the novel, the
failure of the idealists who could not cope with the negative elements in their environment, was a novelty in Mexican fiction.
Azuela's liberal ideas, which can hardly be noticed in *María Luisa,*
pervade *Los fracasados* and give significance to the action. The
conservative elements in the town, represented by the alliance
of the rich *hacendados,* the clergy, and the corrupted politicians,
cannot be conquered by the idealist Reséndez. Nevertheless, his
failure is not as tragic as that of Father Cabezudo, who has to
fight against the ignorance and stupidity of his parishioners.

Azuela, back from medical school, wanted to write a novel
about life in a small town. With this in mind he set out in search
of material. He did not take long in finding it. One early morning,
when he was returning home from attending a patient, he went
into the town's church. There the priest, whom Azuela recognized, was in the middle of a strong sermon against liberalism.
"At that time," Azuela later recollected, "my Jacobinism was past
its critical period and I was in my convalescence; instead of finding
the pastor disagreeable and hateful, I was captivated by his religious passion, his fervor, his speech in good faith, his neat
thoughts and, especially, his bravery in expressing his ideas without subterfuge and with great vigor." [15] In the priest the novelist
recognized the ideal person for his work: a frustrated idealist, a
pathetic figure preaching in the desert. "When the minister came
down from his sacred pulpit, in the midst of the confused rumor-
ing of the people kneeling and waiting for the mass, his divine
words still resounded in the high church ceiling, and it seemed to
me that they had an empty sound." [16]

Besides the ideological conflict between the politicians and the clergymen, there is a contrast between good and bad: some of the characters like Reséndez, Consuelo, and Father Martínez are good, intelligent, and understanding; others, like Dr. Caracas, the daughters of doña Recareda, and Father Delgado, are evil and ignorant. The novelist has not yet learned the technique of creating real characters that stand out from the group, and not just simple types like those found here, such as the small-town lawyer, the political boss, the judge, the local doctor, the secretary of the city council, and the parish priest. Nevertheless, the ability to characterize that is so much admired in the novels of the later periods is already apparent. Father Cabezudo, for instance, after preaching a whole lifetime against the liberals, finally realizes that the true enemy is not liberalism, but wickedness itself. The scene in which he discovers this truth is one of the best in the novel. Doña Recareda has plainly misunderstood the minister's admonitions against the liberals. "For we are authorized by you, *señor cura*," she says, "to kill the liberals if the act is of benefit to our soul and increases God's glory." [17]

In Father Martínez, Azuela has created an original character. He is not like the typical priest in most of the novels of the period. Although a friend of the liberals, he is not a renegade. In the novel his function is to demonstrate that not all priests are reactionaries. No less interesting is the lawyer Reséndez, a character drawn from life, according to the author. In Reséndez, Azuela portrayed his friend José Becerra, the lawyer, poet, and revolutionary who later was instrumental in determining the novelist's participation in the war against Huerta and later Carranza.

The plot of *Los fracasados* unfolds without undue complications. Reséndez, upon completing his law studies in Guadalajara, accepts a position in a small town of the state as secretary to the city council. He arrives with a great deal of enthusiasm, ready to put into practice the ideal of social justice he has learned from his professors. He soon discovers that there is little in common between the classroom and the real world, for he has to fight against powerful reactionary forces controlled by persons without scruples who are ready to sacrifice their principles in order to keep their power. Reséndez is defeated through trickery, and after an attempt to kill him fails, he escapes with his life. There is, of course, a secondary intrigue. Reséndez falls in love with Consuelo, the daughter of one of the men in control of the town, the *hacendado* don Agapito. The fact that Consuelo turns out to be the daughter of Father Martínez (conceived before he had become a priest) shows that Azuela had not yet learned the subtleties of his art.

More important than the plot is the criticism Azuela makes of the social institutions that existed in a small town typical of the Díaz era. The contemporary writer Agustín Yáñez has done the same thing in his novel *Al filo del agua* (1947).[18] Although these two novels differ in technique and style, there are certain similarities between them. The theme, the scenery, and the characters are the same. The conflict between liberals and conservatives is the same. In both works there is an identical religious parade, in defiance of the Laws of Reform. The town where the events of *Al filo del agua* take place is very much like the Alamos of *Los fracasados*. The society depicted in both novels is that which existed in Mexico's provincial towns just before the Revolution of 1910. In Azuela's novel the action takes place in 1906; in Yáñez', in 1909. The excellent work of Yáñez, written forty years later, is much superior to Azuela's in both style and technique. Nevertheless, life in a small town as painted by Azuela has the charm of being a first impression of events as seen by a contemporary while Yáñez' novel, although much more artistic, is a re-creation of a period gone by, of a society seen at a distance through the eyes of the imagination.

Azuela's strongest point, in this and subsequent novels, is the vigor and force with which he presents the problems of that society he knew so well. His ardent liberalism and his impatience with human stupidity come through with clearness and precision. Attorney Reséndez, the hero of the novel, realizes that Mexican life under the Díaz regime needs to be improved, as it devalues intelligence in favor of audacity and intrigue. Those in power are mediocre, unlearned, and without talent, but daring and unscrupulous.

In spite of the severe criticism of the Díaz regime, Azuela was not punished for the publication of *Los fracasados*. Just a few years before the novelist Heriberto Frías had been court-martialed and condemned to death (although the sentence was not carried out) for publishing his novel *Tomóchic* in the newspaper *El Demócrata* of Mexico City in 1893. The novel described the ruthless destruction of an Indian village in northern Mexico by a regiment of Díaz' soldiers. The wide publicity it gained throughout the nation led to its suppression and to the punishment of its author, who was an officer in that same army that had destroyed the town of Tomóchic. Was it that the attitude of the Díaz government toward adverse criticism had changed between 1893 and 1908, or was it that Azuela's novel went unnoticed by the critics and the public? The latter explanation seems more plausible, as Azuela himself complained that his novel had been noticed by only a few critics. He received letters from Victoriano Salado Alvarez and Amado Nervo. The only notice that appeared in newspapers or periodicals was that of Ricardo Arenales in the literary review, *Contemporáneos,* of Monterrey in 1910.[19]

Compared to the latter novels written by Azuela, *Los fracasados* is relatively unimportant; however, it marks the end, as he says, of his period as an amateur in the art of the novel. The few favorable comments he received were enough to make him decide to dedicate himself seriously to the writing of fiction.

V Mala Yerba

Mala yerba (1909),[20] translated into English by Anita Brenner under the title *Marcela* (1932), is doubtless Azuela's best novel of this early period. The greatest improvement is to be found in the technique employed. For the first time he is able to skillfully blend human actions and descriptions of nature. When one of the peons is assassinated, the storm that rages turns into a symbol of the social explosion that is to envelop the whole country. The descriptions of nature, although given symbolic meaning, faithfully reproduce the Mexican landscape, giving the novel an authentic note. The same can be said about the descriptions of the people, their daily life, and their speech. To really capture the spirit of life in the country, Azuela said, "It is not necessary to have been born on the ranch, but it is essential to be thoroughly acquainted with the environment, to know the people first-hand, especially at an early age, when we can receive vigorous and rich impressions."[21] And indeed Azuela, to write *Mala yerba,* drew on his experiences as a boy on his father's ranch, where he became acquainted with the peons, cowboys, and servants.

The story told by Azuela in this novel is one of social protest. While in Lagos, serving as municipal doctor, he had the opportunity to become acquainted with numerous legal cases. "I was able," he said in an interview, "to find out about all the crimes committed by the *hacendados.* How astonishing the number of cases! An *hacendado* could kill a peon under the least pretext, or even without one. That, of course, took place during the days of Porfirio Díaz. Things are different now. Oh, how many crimes!" [22] One of these crimes gave him material for his novel. Going over the proceedings of a murder trial one day, Azuela became interested in the case and decided to use it for the novel that he was planning to write about rural life. It was the case of a rich *hacendado* who had murdered his stableman and his own young and beautiful wife after accusing her of infidelity. In *Mala yerba* Julián Andrade, the decadent *hacendado,* orders that his stableman, Gertrudis, be killed because Gertrudis is the lover of Marcela, a young girl that Julián desires. At the end of the novel Julián kills Marcela, with his own hands, while she is unconscious and thus cannot defend herself.

It was not the first time that this story had appeared in Mexican literature. Before 1909 it had been used by Victoriano Salado Alvarez in his short story "De autos," [23] and by Amado Nervo in his novelette *Pascual Aguilera* (1896). Azuela himself had used the plot, although without development, in his short story "De mi tierra" (1903), in which Teodora, a well-developed girl of sixteen, is seduced by the *hacendado* just before she marries her sweetheart Macedonio, one of the peons.

The similarities between Nervo's novelette and Azuela's novel are limited to the nature of the characters, since the outcome of *Pascual Aguilera* is entirely different. However, Refugio (the heroine in Nervo's story) is very much like Marcela; Santiago, Refugio's sweetheart, could be a brother of Gertrudis; and Pascual Aguilera, Nervo's protagonist, belongs to the same social class and has the same attitudes toward the men and women of the hacienda as Julián Andrade. The similarities, however, end here. Nervo's style is *modernista,* and even the peons and rancheros speak like educated Mexicans. For this reason, the dialogues are artificial, not suited to the characters. On the other hand, Azuela's peons and people of the countryside speak and behave like the typical inhabitants of the region, and, in Azuela's novels, the sense of injustice is ever present. He is constantly protesting against the corrupt judges who side with the *caciques* against the defenseless peons. From this point of view, *Mala yerba* could be considered as an introduction to *Los de abajo*. These injustices, tolerated by the Díaz government and so well depicted by Azuela in this novel, help us to understand the causes of the revolution.

In the development of Azuela's narrative technique, *Mala yerba* represents a moment of transition. Still found here are the Naturalistic elements characteristic of his first novels. Marcela, for example, is still characterized as a woman (very much like María Luisa) who is dominated by her environment: "Over Marcela weighed the tremendous power of the arrogant breed of debauchers who were never denounced by their victims." [24] Throughout the novel are found descriptions of the customs of the people of that region which Azuela knew so well. The most important *costumbrista* scenes are the horse race and the bull fight. The scene where Tía Poncianita appears (chapter XI) is a true *cuadro costumbrista,* reminiscent of the best pages of Luis G. Inclán, the author of *Astucia*. The lively dialogue between the peons and the women from the town (chapter XII) is an excellent re-creation of the popular speech of that part of Jalisco called Los Altos, where the novel takes place. [25]

A new element in this novel is the appearance of the ironic attitude, which is to predominate in future works. The description of the indolent judge, a judge not unlike those that appear in the novels of the Venezuelan Rómulo Gallegos, serves to break the tension which results from the nature of the tragedy. After Marcela's death, which would be the logical end of the novel, Azuela adds a short chapter which has the sole function of satirizing the judge and justice in general under the Díaz regime. The judge, who has been unable to make justice prevail and punish the guilty party, says to his secretary: "I am very sleepy and I am going to bed. Tomorrow, very early, come to my house to milk the goats. And I also want you to pull up from the furrow a few sweet potatoes for my María Engracia. Good night, don Petronilo." [26]

The most important aspect of this novel, however, is the revelation of the author's social consciousness. Although in the previous novels and short stories this social awareness is not absent, it is in *Mala yerba* that for the firt time the mixed attitude of indignation and sentimentalism disappears completely. The solid tone of indignation, without any sentimentality (and this is what distinguishes Azuela from Federico Gamboa), makes *Mala yerba* the best novel of the early period. After *Los de abajo* it is perhaps Azuela's most popular novel. The translation by Anita Brenner made it famous in the English-speaking world. Azuela himself had an obvious preference for this work, as demonstrated by the fact that during his latter years he wrote a sequel to it, *Esa sangre,* published after his death.

During the same year that *Mala yerba* was published there appeared a short story, "Avichuelos negros," in which Azuela satirizes the customs and ideas of small-town people. María is not permitted by the morally overzealous women, the "black ugly birds," to take care of her lover, who is dying of tuberculosis, because she is not legally married. In her absence he dies and the rats gnaw his feet.

VI Sin Amor

Sin amor (Without Love), although published in 1912,[27] was probably written before *Mala yerba*. It follows slavishly the technique of the French novel of the period and is therefore less representative of Azuela's style. The author himself recognized that he had not been true to his nature. "There is in *Sin amor,*" he tells us, "something strange to my being, something that clashes with my spontaneous and even rude frankness. This strangeness is not found, I believe, in the subject matter, but in the form in which it is expressed." [28]

In the subject matter, to be sure, there is nothing original. It has to do with the social aspirations that a middle-class mother, Lidia, has for her daughter Ana María. Wishing to be accepted by the social circle they consider the highest in the small town, that is, the group formed by the rich, they sacrifice their dignity and their honor. Ana María finally succeeds in marrying the richest man in town, Ramón Torralba, by sacrificing her happiness, for it is a marriage of convenience, without love.

To make the tragedy of María stand out, Azuela develops, on parallel lines, the story of a friend, Julia Ponce, who marries a poor officer and is thus able to retain her dignity. This aspect of the novel, however, is not well developed. The marriage of Julia and Enrique is a very obvious situation, inserted in the novel with the only purpose of giving emphasis to the vulgar and disastrous marriage of Ana María to Ramón.

Azuela attributed his failure this time to a lack of objectivity on his part in the presentation of the problems of the middle class. "Perhaps," he said, "my being too close to the middle class prohibits my looking at it objectively and my studying it in all its aspects. My observations are therefore expressed with passion and perhaps with injustice. Novels about the middle class are the ones that I enjoy least, and I have shown this unsympathetic attitude with my own *Sin amor* by not publishing a second edition." [29]

The novel is very much like *Los fracasados*. The action takes place in a small town, the same Lagos de Moreno of the former novel. Nevertheless, in *Sin amor* there are very few direct references to the town, and the descriptions of the landscape are not as vivid as in *Mala yerba*. The novel is, undoubtedly, the least realistic of this period. In the style, Azuela shows the influence of the *modernistas*. This is the way he describes a nightfall: "It had become dark; twilight ended in a final flicker: like a Rembrandt oil painting that fuses in a Ruelas etching." [30] Julio Ruelas at that time was the illustrator of the *Revista Moderna* of Mexico City, a literary periodical published by Amado Nervo, Jesús E. Valenzuela, and other *modernistas*.

No less artificial in *Sin amor* are the characters. Although taken from life, they are stereotypes which never seem to become real persons. Don Salustiano represents the greedy moneylender. Nacho de la Rosa is a frustrated poet. Escolástica (the name itself is an abstraction), represents the hypocritical woman who pretends to be interested in culture. Canales is the attorney who has failed. Don Salvador is the trustworthy bartender who knows how to keep the secrets of the dandies. Only the young feminine characters, Ana María and Julia, receive special attention. They are well characterized and become women who live and have human warmth. This is, perhaps, the only advance in technique that Azuela demonstrates in this novel: his ability to create acceptable feminine characters. Otherwise, omitted are the criticism of the social institutions, his strong, vivid, regional style, and his fine descriptions of the Mexican landscape. There is a wide difference between *Sin amor* and *Mala yerba*. If the latter is a definite success, the former has to be classed as a failure. This failure is due, perhaps, to the fact that Azuela forgets himself and tries to imitate European novelists. As he himself says, *Sin amor* is an imitation of the novel *El pueblo gris* by the Spanish novelist Santiago Rusiñol.

Sin amor closes a period in Azuela's development as a novelist. "With this novel," he wrote, "ended the first cycle of my production, at the moment when the nation was beginning to tremble with the revolution of Madero in the North." [31]

CHAPTER 3

The Novels of Revolution

I Andres Perez, maderista

WITH *Andrés Pérez, maderista* (1911)[1] a new cycle begins in the development of Mariano Azuela as a novelist. He abandons the techniques predominant in Mexican fiction at the end of the nineteenth century and still in use during the first decade of the twentieth. Azuela is therefore the first Mexican novelist to try new techniques, new forms, and new subjects. There is a noticeable change between his previous novels and those written after 1911. In his new mode of expression dialogue predominates over description; characterization is achieved less through direct portrayal than through dialogue and action. The point of view changes from the omniscient narrator to the first person; the action is observed now through the eyes of a character in the novel and not by the author. The world of the novel changes from that of the small-town middle-class environment or the rural society at the hacienda to that of a nation engaged in a civil war. Thus, with *Andrés Pérez, maderista* Azuela creates what has since come to be known in literary history as "the Novel of the Revolution."

It is not until *Los de abajo* appears in 1915, however, that a completely new novel is born. In *Andrés Pérez, maderista* the familiar types are still found: the newspaperman (Don Cuco), the *cacique* (Colonel Hernández), the stableman (Vicente). Only two of the characters, Andrés Pérez and Toño Reyes, come to life. They are given a sense of reality by the striking difference in the outcome of their destinies. Toño, the idealist, dies fighting for a better society; Andrés, the opportunist, can think of nothing else but his personal well-being. He survives to enjoy life with Toño's wife, thus betraying not only the revolution but the memory of his best friend. The latter action is not dramatized— it is only suggested at the end of the novel. This method of structuring the novel with the characters in opposition is to be found frequently in Azuela's works. In *Los de abajo* Andrés and Toño are replaced by Luis Cervantes and Solís.

Because of its novelty, the theme introduced in *Andrés Pérez, maderista* constitutes a departure from the traditional novel. Azuela uses a theme, the betrayal of the revolution, taken from contemporary history, and dramatizes it for the first time in the novel. It reappears in *Los de abajo,* and, indeed, in several of his later novels. The revolution, according to this eyewitness, was betrayed by the former rulers, the *porfiristas* in disguise. Azuela reveals the manner in which the revolution fell into the hands of the former *caciques.* Colonel Hernández, the town's political boss under Díaz, and Don Cuco, the newspaperman, both of them dyed-in-the-wool *porfiristas,* jump on the bandwagon as soon as they see that the revolution has triumphed. They immediately put on the uniform of the revolutionaries and are thus able to continue at the head of the town's government.

In this novel Azuela makes excellent use of humor and satire to ridicule the actions of the pseudo-revolutionaries. Andrés Pérez, the antihero, becomes the head of the revolutionary faction through a series of errors worthy of a comic opera. Without any convictions, without any desire to lead the revolt against Díaz, without any social consciousness, he becomes the leader of the rebel army. As a result, the followers of Díaz, in disguise, are able to sabotage the revolution and reap gains for their political party and for the conservatives. Only Don Octavio, who in the novel represents the author, as his ideology is similar to that of Azuela, realizes the contradictory role that circumstances have foisted upon Andrés.

The novel is saved from becoming a farce by the pessimistic tone associated with the actions of Toño Reyes, whose tragic end is a vain sacrifice. Toño's efforts on behalf of Madero and his ideals are belittled by the actions of Andrés and by his own death. After the victory, the *caciques* whom Toño had fought, continue ruling. Colonel Hernández, now a general, "because there is no higher rank," cynically relates how timely the uprising has been, as it has coincided with Díaz' departure to Europe and has therefore saved their positions.

Although a short novel, *Andrés Pérez, maderista* is a key work in the development of Azuela as a writer of fiction, and, indeed, as the initiation of a genre that was to become one of the most important in Mexican literature.

II Los Caciques

In *Mala yerba,* Azuela had painted the injustices committed against the peons by the feudal lords of the *haciendas.* In *Los caciques,* a novel written in 1914 but not published until 1917, he deals with the crimes of the *caciques* in the towns.[2] Both novels help to dramatize and highlight forcibly the causes of the revolution, and therefore they can be very helpful in the understanding of *Los de abajo* as well as of other novels of the same nature.

The action in *Mala yerba* takes place during the last years of the long Díaz era; that of *Andrés Pérez, maderista,* during the years that the revolution begins; and that of *Los caciques* during the short period that Madero occupied the presidency of Mexico. The novel ends right after Madero is assassinated and his followers take up arms to fight the hated Huerta government. Although published after *Los de abajo,* the events it depicts took place before those of the later novel. When Villa took the city of Zacatecas, Azuela put the finishing touches on *Los caciques.*

This novel is an exposé of the methods used by the city bosses to exploit the people. The characters here created serve to dramatize that idea. As in some of his other novels, the plot in *Los caciques* is just an excuse to dramatize the conflict between the rulers of the town and their victims. It is interesting to note that here these "victims" do not belong to the lower but to the middle class. Don Juanito Viñas is a small business man; Rodríguez is a store clerk; Don Juanito's wife, Elena, and his daughter, Esperanza, are typical middle-class women. The conflict is not between the rich and the poor, the upper and the lower classes, but between the *caciques* and the members of the middle class who refuse to submit and accept their system. The lower class, in this novel, is painted in somber tones. The meeting of the political club, sarcastically called "20 de Noviembre," (the date the revolution began) is a farcical scene. "The first act was to name committees. The Rat was placed in charge of the balloons; Pedrito, a fellow with a chimpanzee face and covered with soot from head to feet, in charge of the gunpowder; the Pig, in charge of lanterns and torches."[3] Don Timoteo, the leader of the revolutionaries, is nothing but a caricature, a clown; *El Puerco* (The

Pig), another one of the leaders, is a traitor who would sell his own comrades for a few coins. Azuela's disillusion with the outcome of the revolution is beginning to show in this scene, as well as in the portrayal of the followers of the movement.

The plot of *Los caciques* is straightforward. Don Juanito, with great sacrifice, has been able to save twenty thousand pesos. Advised by the rich merchants, Del Llano brothers, he invests this money in the construction of some model homes. Not having enough money to finish the project, he is dispossessed of his investment by Del Llano brothers. As a result, Don Juanito becomes ill and finally dies, never losing his faith in the good intentions of his so-called protectors, who knew beforehand that he was unable to get sufficient money to finish the homes. Thus, Don Juanito becomes the symbol of the good, innocent man who is the victim of greed and evil. He is contrasted with the most respected of the Del Llano brothers, Ignacio, a voracious despoiler of the people.

The second victim, Rodríguez, also belongs to the middle class. As an intellectual, an idealist, and a dreamer, he is hated by both the *caciques* and the revolutionaries. He is very much like Reséndez in *Los fracasados,* that is, a symbol of the misunderstood idealist. But he is also a chronic pessimist, aware of the stupidity of the masses. He believes, however, that in spite of their stupidity the masses are preferable to the decadent, dishonest, and autocratic *caciques.* He, like Toño in *Andrés Pérez, maderista,* pays with his life in defense of his ideas. The *caciques* order him shot to death as his dissenting ideas are beginning to have influence in the town.

One striking feature of this novel is the absence of descriptions of nature. Of his novels, *Los caciques* is perhaps the one that has the least description, becoming almost pure action. At the same time, there is no single protagonist. Don Juanito, the only one who appears throughout the novel, does not have the stature of a hero. He is a weakling, a small-town business man who not only does not fight for his rights, but even praises his oppressors. Rodríguez, who could have been a true hero, is murdered halfway through the novel. Among the female characters the only one that stands out is Esperanza. The others are mere symbols, as are the rest of the characters. Don Ignacio represents the typical small-town *cacique;* his brother Jeremías is a venal and libidinous curate;

their sister Teresa is a woman who has lost all touch with humanity. One of her favorite sayings is: "If the poor have no corn or beans, they eat *nopales* [prickly cactuses] . . . And they are so happy!"[4]

In *Los caciques* plot development is made unobtrusive in order to bring out with force the central theme, the injustice of the *caciques*. The dramatization of these injustices is so vivid that the armed revolt with which the novel ends is made to seem justified. Otherwise, the novel, especially with respect to technique, adds nothing to Azuela's development as a narrator. The novel is the simple dramatization of life in a provincial Mexican town at the time when the great conflict was to explode. It is written, however, with great vigor, indignation, and emotive force. In his desire to expose these injustices, however, Azuela falls into the error of unduly simplifying the structure of that society which he depicts, as well as the actions of the persons that live in his novel. Nevertheless, the reader is made to sympathize with the victims and denounce the *caciques*.

The novel was rewritten for the stage by the author himself and was published in 1938 under the title *Del Llano Hnos., S. en C.* (Del Llano Bros., Commindite).

III Los de abajo

Los de abajo,[5] Azuela's masterpiece and one of the great Mexican novels, appeared precisely a hundred years after *El Periquillo Sarniento* of José Joaquín Fernández de Lizardi, the first romance published in the country. If the novel by Lizardi revived a lost genre, the picaresque novel, Azuela's work initiated another, the novel of the revolution.

Los de abajo is not, as might be thought, the result of hasty writing done while away in the field or in a hotel room. The ideas embodied in the novel can be easily traced in previous works by Azuela. The title, "Los de abajo," which has accounted for a great deal of the popularity of the novel, first appeared in *Los fracasados*. About the hero of the early novel, Azuela says: "What could he have found during his busy life except the olympic disdain of the upper classes [*los de arriba*] and the indifference and meanness of the lower classes [*los de abajo*]?"[6] Some of the characters of *Los de abajo* had already appeared in previous works. Camila, the girl in love with Cervantes who, against her will, ends up as Demetrio's lover and is finally mur-

dered, had appeared in the short story "En derrota" (1904).
There she is the daughter of the hacienda's *mayordomo* and the
object of Juan's passion. The following scene foreshadows one in
Los de abajo: "But he [Juan], with his head down, was contemplating her [Camila] with ecstasy on the surface of the spring
whose blue water reflected her image."⁷ In *Los de abajo* when
Camila appears for the first time the image of the blue water is
associated with her. Demetrio, wounded and very thirsty, asks
for water. "A very kind young girl brought a gourd full of blue
water."⁸ Demetrio drinks the water with eagerness and, lifting
his eyes, contemplates Camila, not with love, like Juan, but with
gratefulness.⁹

The central character in *Los de abajo,* Demetrio Macías, first
comes to life in the person of Gertrudis, the stableman in the novel
Mala yerba. He reappears in *Andrés Pérez, maderista,* as Vicente,
another stableman. In the same novel, the hero Toño Reyes
foreshadows the poet Solís, who in *Los de abajo* has the function
of expressing Azuela's social and political ideas. Toño's friend,
Andrés Pérez, reappears in *Los de abajo* with the name Luis
Cervantes. It is only among the secondary characters, such as El
Güero Margarito and La Pintada, that new creations are found,
for even the soldiers who ride under Demetrio's orders appeared
before in *Mala yerba.* It is obvious, therefore, that the reader must
look elsewhere for what is new in *Los de abajo.*

The plot can hardly be called original, as it repeats the same
structure Azuela had used in *Andrés Pérez, maderista,* a series of
scenes and episodes. Although presented without any order, they
are unified by the presence of Demetrio. The novel opens with
the triumph of Demetrio over the federal soldiers in the Cañón
de Juchipila and ends with his death in exactly the same place. The
organization of the material, however, does not follow a pre-
arranged scheme. The novel, like the revolution itself, like the
men that make up the rebel forces, has no definite plan. However,
behind this complete lack of order can be detected a form that is
not at variance with the events narrated. The fact that Azuela
made use of this apparently chaotic form, which in the end turned
out to be the most appropriate for the subject developed, demonstrates that he possessed a narrative talent which placed him above
most of the novelists who treated the theme of the revolution.

In *Los de abajo* Azuela abandons the techniques of the European novelists and creates a new novel, genuinely Mexican, admirably adapted to give expression to the theme. Its creation was significant in the development of the Spanish American novel, as it set a trend toward the use of national subjects, characters, and environments.

One of the characteristics that gives *Los de abajo* originality is the harmonious relationship that prevails between the dialogue and the descriptions of nature. At the same time, each action is made to stand out by associating with it a short description of the landscape:

At sunset, amid the flames dyeing the sky with vivid, variegated colors, a group of shacks appeared in the dusk, in a clearing surrounded by blue mountains. Demetrio ordered them to carry him there.[10]

The men threw out their chests as if to breathe the widening horizon, the immensity of the sky, the blue of the mountains and the fresh air, fragrant with the aromas of the sierras. They spurred their horses to a gallop as if in that unbridled race they could claim possession of the earth.[11]

Frequently a few strokes are sufficient to draw a complete picture of the landscape, animated with the presence of a few animals:

It was a silent and prudently joyous dawn. A thrush chirped timidly in the ash tree. The animals in the corral treaded upon the refuse from the stubble. The pig grunted its somnolence. The pale orange colored tinge of the sun appeared, and the last little star went out.[12]

At the same time, Azuela is able, with great skill, to emphasize man's violent actions by setting them off against nature's peaceful serenity. The novel ends with a powerful description of this kind. Demetrio's death is framed in glorious surroundings:

The smoke from the rifles has not disappeared yet. Locusts chant their serene, mysterious song. Doves sing tenderly in the crannies of the rocks. Cows graze peacefully.

The sierra has a festive appearance. Over its inaccessible peaks the white mist settles like a snowy veil over the head of a bride.

At the foot of a huge hollow, as sumptuous as the portico of an old cathedral, Demetrio Macías, with his eyes forever fixed, continues to aim his rifle . . .[13]

Man's ignoble actions are also counterbalanced against appropriate descriptions of nature. When Luis Cervantes, revealing his
low moral fiber, tries to convince Camila that she should accept
Macías as a lover, the disillusioned young girl, who loves Luis,
bursts into tears. The novelist ends the scene with these words:
"Among the reeds, the frogs sang the implacable melancholy of the
hour. Swaying from a dry twig, a wild dove wept also." [14]

Los de abajo is a truly representative novel of Mexico, just as
Doña Bárbara by Rómulo Gallegos is representative of Venezuela,
and *El mundo es ancho y ajeno* (*Broad and Alien Is the World*)
by Ciro Alegría is representative of Perú. By reading *Los de
abajo,* Mexico's struggle for liberty can be understood a little
better. The reader identifies with the men who did the fighting,
with their aspirations and their shortcomings. The novel reveals the
author's rebellious spirit as well as his desire to see a better Mexico
evolve from the struggle—a Mexico in which social justice and an
improved way of life for the underdog may prevail.

Not satisfied with having treated this problem in *Los de abajo,*
Azuela comes back to the same theme in his subsequent novels,
such as *Los caciques, Las moscas* (*The Flies*), and *Las tribulaciones de una familia decente,* the last one closing the cycle of the
novels of the revolution. If to these are added *Domitilo quiere ser
diputado* (a short novelette; 1918), and the short stories "De
como al fin lloró Juan Pablo" (1918), "El jurado" (1922)
("The Jury"), "Y ultimadamente . . ." (1924), as well as the
unpublished "El caso López Romero" (1916),[15] there emerges
a complete panorama of the revolutionary movement from beginning to end. In these works Azuela depicts the causes of the
revolt, the savage fighting, the triumph (material, but not spiritual), and the failures. In a word, here is the epic struggle of a
people who arise after a long sleep. The power of these novels
and short stories, especially that of *Los de abajo,* is derived from
the great, sincere love that the author had for his land and its
people and from the emotions he felt upon contemplating the
great conflagration, a conflagration that moved him to the depths
of his soul.

IV Las moscas

The Flies (*Las moscas,* 1918)[16] is more a series of scenes and
sketches unified by the theme of the Mexican Revolution than a

novel. Their dynamic nature is similar to that found in Orozco's sketches, which treat the same subject from the same point of view. The first part of the novel takes place in a provincial capital in the central region of Mexico; the second is a vivid and at the same time humorous trip in one of the many trains in which the *villistas* withdrew to the north after their defeat at Celaya. The work ends with the painting of several scenes in the station and city of Irapuato, where the train has stopped before continuing north.

There is no formal plot in this novel, and there are no heroes. The characters, or rather groups of characters, appear and disappear. It is an endless procession of generals (Malacara), judges (Mr. Ríos), government employees (Reyes Téllez, Moralitos), school principals (Neftalí), unemployed teachers (Aurora and Raquel), former *porfiristas* (Don Sinforoso), loose women (Cachucha, Manuela), and even "teachers of energy" (Don Rodolfo); all of them, like flies, are in search of food and with no other aim but to survive. "Our political party," one of them says, "is that one which feeds us." [17]

The novel does not have a rigid structure. The scenes follow each other naturally, in chronological order. Often the scenes include several groups of people who act at the same time, as in the opening pages at the railroad station. The same thing happens at the end, in Irapuato, where Azuela has skillfully painted the disorder and confusion that result when an army has to withdraw in defeat.

The absence of a character representing the pessimistic intellectual, through which Azuela usually gives expression to his own ideas, is noticeable in *Las moscas.* It seems that Azuela here for a moment forgot his social philosophy and concentrated only in the painting of the government employee who cares about nothing except his own well-being. If that was his aim, he succeeded. The prevalent humor and satire give this novelette a dimension that unifies it and gives it an artistic touch. *Las moscas* may not be a great novel, but it certainly is a great canvas on which Azuela has preserved an aspect of the revolution. The picture may not be edifying, but it certainly was painted with great realism and a critical attitude. The last scene, of Villa in defeat, is a magnificent sketch of that fallen hero.

V Domitilo quiere ser diputado

Domitilo quiere ser diputado (1918)[18] is a long short story rather than a novel. As in *Las moscas* and the short stories "El caso López Romero" (written in 1916 but not published until 1960)[19] and *De como al fin lloró Juan Pablo* (1918) Azuela here makes use of a single incident dealing with the revolution. It deals with the trick the treasurer of the town plays on the rich to make them contribute to the general's war fund. The author does not fail to take advantage of the opportunity to show how the treasurer benefits in the transaction. This simple anecdote, inconsequential in itself, is well suited to bring out the character's selfish motives. Domitilo's father, don Serapio, has a simple philosophy: "To live means to be able to adapt oneself to the circumstances." [20] For Don Serapio adapting oneself to the circumstances means collaborating with the government that is in power, regardless of the political philosophy it may represent. He himself has been *porfirista* with Don Porfirio, *maderista* with Madero, villista with Villa, and *carrancista* with Carranza. Why should a man have any scruples about changing from party to party? His astuteness contrasts with the stupidity of his son Domitilo. Don Serapio's ambition is to make his son a representative in Congress, although he knows Domitilo is incapable of holding such a position.

In the figure of General Xicoténcatl Robespierre Cebollino, provisional governor of the town, Azuela has painted a caricature of the extravagant, as well as conceited, *carrancista* leader. At the end it is revealed that he had been, like Don Serapio, a collaborator of Huerta, but throughout the story he has tried to impress those who surround and adulate him with his liberal and even radical ideas.

Apart from the incisive satire against pseudo-revolutionaries, especially the followers of Carranza, and against turncoats, this novelette adds little to the development of the author's narrative technique.

VI Las tribulaciones de una familia decente

With *Las tribulaciones de una familia decente* (1918)[21] Azuela closes the cycle of the novels of the revolution initiated with *Andrés Pérez, maderista* in 1911. In it he continues to depict the ill effects of the struggle. He relates the events that took place in Mexico City in 1916 and 1917 under the Carranza administration, or rather "misadministration," if Azuela is to be believed. Since he was a sincere man and an eyewitness to the events he describes, his work has value as a historical document, that is, a historical document presenting the facts from the point of view of a chronicler unsympathetic to Carranza.

In *Las tribulaciones* Azuela does see the revolution, as in *Los de abajo,* from the perspective of the underdog. In fact, the underdogs are painted without pity; they are savage hordes which roam the streets of the capital, robbing, killing, pillaging, and destroying everything that crosses their path. The action is seen from the point of view of a middle-class family (*"una familia decente"*), the Vázquez Prado—Procopio and Agustinita and their children Francisco José, César, Berta, and Lulú. Leaving their native state, Zacatecas, they take refuge in the capital, thinking that there they are safe from the destructive revolution. But the revolution engulfs the capital itself, and the Vázquez Prado family respite soon comes to an end. Their tribulations and how they solve their problems are the subject of the novel.

It cannot be said that the revolution is the theme of *Las tribulaciones,* although it serves as a background upon which the events unfold, and the fate of the characters is intrinsically bound to the outcome of the struggle. The real theme is the agony that the family must endure in order to adapt itself to a new environment. Procopio's triumph (this is the title of the second part of the novel) consists of his determination to go to work just like a common employee. Having lost his means of livelihood he has to earn his daily bread with his own hands, something a member of a "decent" family is not supposed to do.

But not all the members of this decent family are like Procopio. Except for the younger daughter Lulú, who is very much like her father and goes to work in an office, the others refuse to soil their hands. This social readjustment is, of course, a direct consequence of the revolution. César, the younger son and narrator in the first part of the novel, puts it this way: "This long period of revolutionary administrations and even the pre-constitutional government which now afflicts us have been like a painful Calvary through which we have been ascending without let-up and purging ourselves a thousand and one times not only of our sins but of those of all our ancestors." [22]

In this novel Azuela does not criticize the revolution itself, but the fact that it fell into the hands of bandits like Pascual (Berta's husband) and General Covarrubias, painted as a common thief who saw in the revolution a rich mine that he could exploit. His deeds, which would otherwise be punished with a prison sentence, would now be rewarded with a high position in the government, or a senate seat, or an ambassadorship in a foreign country. The General's name even became famous. But where? "His name became popular, not in the fields of battle, but in the gambling houses and the bawdyhouses; a name that had been forged with the blood of his defenseless victims; but notorious enough to come to the attention of the *C. Primer Jefe*,[23] who knew how to distinguish and even reward such accomplishments with the best positions in his government." [24] Azuela, a strong follower of the Constitutional party, could not forgive Carranza for the favoritism he bestowed upon such drones as General Covarrubias. This attitude predominates throughout the novel. There are no humorous scenes, as in *Las moscas* or *Domitilo* . . . to mitigate the tragic unfolding of the events. Instead, there is a sense of indignation, even rage, because of the indignant and unjust acts committed in the name of the revolution, both by the unrestrained troops and the unworthy officers and even leaders.

After *Los de abajo* this novel is perhaps the best picture of the revolution done by Azuela. The plot, except for the unexpected and unrealistic death of Pascual, is one of the best in Azuela's repertoire. Some of the characters (Agustinita, Procopio, Berta, Pascual) are well depicted. Others, like Lulú, her sweetheart Archibaldo, and the poet Francisco José, although not forcefully drawn, are still believable. And even some of the minor characters, like the go-between Tabardillo and the lecherous Don Ulpiano Pío, although repugnant, are painted with a firm hand.

In the second part of the novel, especially, there are some highly emotive scenes, such as the dinner scene in Pascual's house, and the visit of the latter to the Vázquez Prado family with the purpose of despoiling them of the real estate they had kept in their home town. No less interesting are the scenes where Azuela describes the ravaging acts of the soldiers, as seen through the eyes of Lulú and César while taking a walk downtown. It is because of these pictures that the novel has endured as a social document, since in it Azuela has recorded for posterity the events that took place in Mexico City during those turbulent years when the revolution reached its peak. *Las tribulaciones* . . . is a work that confirms Azuela's often repeated maxim: "I write what I think and what I feel [. . .]. Loyalty and honesty consist, in a writer, of giving his own vision of the world with bravery and sincerity." [25] Azuela may often be wrong in interpreting the facts, but he would never say what he did not feel.

Unfortunately, *Las tribulaciones* . . . has a serious structural flaw. The novel is divided in two parts, widely separated by the change in the point of view. The first part, related by César, reflects a more serene attitude and its tone is rather calm. The second part, in which the events are described by an omniscient narrator, is more violent and the tone restless and uneven. César, Procopio's son, has died, and the book he was writing (the first part of the novel) is finished in a second part by an omniscient narrator. César's unmotivated death is incidentally revealed in the second part. There is no effort to unify these two parts, and the novel could be read as two works except for the fact that the characters are the same and their lives continue to unfold.

CHAPTER 4

An Experiment in Technique

FIVE years went by before Azuela published another novel. Except for the short stories "Paisajes de mi barrio" (1919) and "El jurado" (1922) nothing appeared in print. This does not mean that he was idle. On the contrary, the years between 1918 and 1923 were of great importance in his development as a novelist. He was, as always, busy collecting material for future works, and also experimenting with a new style and new techniques. For several reasons[1] he decided to change his approach to the writing of fiction and also to give up the revolution as a theme. He himself said that he wrote novels in the new form to laugh at the critics. Be that as it may, the fact is that today the experimental novels are considered superior to those he wrote in later years. This break with the novels of the revolution was not, however, as great as he thought it was. The new novels represent, rather, a development of certain techniques which already had appeared in *Andrés Pérez, Los de abajo,* the first part of *Las tribulaciones* and, especially, in the short stories "Y ultimadamente" and "El caso López Romero." From a distance, it is easy to see the similarities, while the differences have diminished. The new technique is noticeable only when comparing these novels and stories with those published after 1937, some of which may have been written earlier, even before the novels of the revolution.

I La Malhora

La Malhora (1923)[2] is a series of scenes unified by the central character, Altagracia (called "La Malhora," the Evil One), a fifteen-year-old prostitute. The slums of Mexico City, where Altagracia's tragedy unfolds, serve as a fitting background and also give unity to the novelette. Azuela has created an environment where desolation and misery prevail. The sordid nature of the slums is emphasized by describing them in terms of lights and shadows: "Abrió. Una franja de luz encendió los baches; estrecha cinta luminosa en el fango negro." ("She opened [the door]. A streak of light lit the street holes; a narrow luminous ribbon over the black mud.")[3] Frequently these realistic descriptions end with a surrealistic image, as can be observed in the following example:

> The electric poles and their festoons are absurd. They extend along the street of a group of wretched shacks that grows smaller in the distance until it licks the dust, until it fuses with the green-gray line at the foot of the hills farther on, near a sky like an eye with a cataract.[4]

Not everything in this novel is new. There are certain recurring elements that make the reader think about some of Azuela's previous works. The Gutiérrez sisters, for whom La Malhora works as a servant for five years, are very much like the Vázquez Prado of *Las tribulaciones*. The protagonist herself, especially in the scenes that take place in the hospital, is very much like the María Luisa of Guadalajara. The *porfirista* general for whom La Malhora also works as a servant, is similar to the generals of that political party who appear in the novels of the revolution. But these resemblances are really very few when compared to the new elements introduced.

La Malhora is the story of Altagracia and her adventures as a servant. Altagracia goes from home to home serving one master after another. This structure is similar to that of the Spanish picaresque novel, in which the hero is a boy of many masters, but the resemblance ends there. *La Malhora* is a somber, tragic novel.

The first episode takes place in the home of an insane but very kind doctor. The surrealistic and absurd nature of this scene is acceptable because the reader knows that the doctor is insane and the world he paints is his world. From the doctor's home Altagracia goes to live as a servant with the prudish Gutiérrez sisters who are able to reform the young prostitute temporarily. After serving them for five years she goes on to the house of a retired general, and Azuela takes this opportunity to describe sarcastically a man who lives in the past and for whom the world has not changed. Altagracia is later interned in a hospital where the doctors tell her that her illness is the result of having been underfed all her life and that there is nothing that medical science can do for her. Here the author severely criticizes doctors and the medical profession. Advised by one of the nurses, Altagracia leaves the hospital and returns to her first profession, to lead a life of vice and live in squalor.

Although the main purpose of the novelist is to depict the miserable life of Altagracia in the slums of Mexico City, there is also a narrative thread. Through the help of La Tapatía, a woman greatly responsible for her misfortunes, Altagracia is wronged by the man who has killed her father. When Altagracia returns to her old neighborhood to avenge herself, she finds La Tapatía living with this man. At this point the novel ends. Azuela himself has said that Altagracia forgives the couple,[5] but the reader is left with the impression that she kills them.

Most of the action in *La Malhora* takes place in the Mexico City slum called Tepito, in the neighborhood of La Bolsa, famous in Mexican literature since the days of Fernández de Lizardi. Azuela faithfully reproduces the habits, speech, and actions of the inhabitants of this part of the city; he knew the area well as he worked there every day taking care of persons like those who appear in the novel.

In technique this novel represents an original contribution to the development of the Mexican novel. *La Malhora* foreshadows novels like *Al filo del agua* (1947) by Agustín Yáñez and *La región más transparente* (1958) by the young Carlos Fuentes.

II El desquite

In *La Malhora* there are reminiscences of the story of María Luisa. Altagracia, in spite of her efforts, is inevitably led to a life of prostitution and crime. In *El desquite (Revenge)*,[6] Azuela's second experimental novel, there are overtones of *Sin amor* in the use of the same theme, but not in its treatment. The style here is that of *La Malhora*. The story is told in a fragmentary, nervous, choppy style. The technique of suggesting instead of telling, of drawing the scenes with blurred strokes, of letting the description stand half finished, is also that of *La Malhora*.

Unfortunately, the technique is wasted on a theme that offers nothing new. As in *Sin amor,* the plot deals with a marriage motivated by avarice. Lenita—like Lidia in the former novel—marries her daughter Lupe to Blas, the richest boor in town. Incompatability is the keynote in this loveless marriage. To complicate matters, they cannot have a son and adopt Blas's little brother, Ricardito, who turns out to be the villain of the story, as he schemes endlessly to deprive his foster mother of her inheritance. Ricardito's tactics, like those of Iago, consist of trying to instill jealousy in his brother's heart. But Blas is no Othello, and Lupe no Desdemona. She is the one who overpowers her husband, inducing him to drink excessively until he dies of alcoholic congestion. The whole town accuses Lupe of having poisoned her husband, although they have no evidence. She is defended by a former sweetheart, Martín, who is able to prove her innocence. After the trial the lawyer marries Lupe, although he no longer loves her. She in turn becomes a dipsomaniac and under the influence of alcohol has hallucinations in which Blas appears to torment her, thus getting his revenge (*desquite*).

The action in the novel takes place in a small town in the interior of Mexico, although the narrator is a doctor living in Mexico City, where some of the scenes take place. This unnecessary shift of locale detracts from the novel, for there are scenes in Mexico City—like the bullfighting scene—which add nothing to the development of the plot. The same thing could be said about the descriptions of the train trips to and from Mexico City. The weak ending is perhaps the novel's greatest flaw. *El desquite* has neither the artistic ending of *The Underdogs* nor the emotive ending of *La Malhora*. The ending, moreover, is ambiguous; it is not known whose revenge is more important, that of Lupe or that of Blas. If it is that of Blas, is he avenging himself for having been murdered or because Lupe did not give him a son? It is not clear, either, if Blas's death was the result of his drinking or if Ricardito, whose name was not even mentioned at the trial, poisoned him. Although Lupe is declared not guilty, no effort is made to determine who killed Blas. The last scenes, where Lupe loses her mind, are not well drawn. Azuela here does not give a realistic picture of Lupe's insanity, nor of the terror she feels when the ghost of Blas appears to her.

It cannot be said that *El desquite* is among Azuela's best efforts. He was not able to present a balanced work, as a disharmony is apparent between technique and subject matter, between theme and expression. His style is less spontaneous than in his other novels dealing with the middle class.

III La Luciérnaga

La Luciérnaga (*The Firefly*) (1932),[7] written in 1926, is the third and last of the experimental novels. With it Azuela is able to master the new technique and produce one of his best novels. The repetition of the theme which first appeared in *Las tribulaciones*—the maladjusted small town family in Mexico City—does not detract from the merit of the novel, since here Azuela is not dealing with the external forces that ruin the family but with internal struggles in the souls of the characters. The world is seen from the point of view of the principal characters, not from that of the omniscient narrator.

If *La Luciérnaga* is similar to *Las tribulaciones* in the theme and to *La Malhora* in the locale, it is like *El desquite* in that the action shifts back and forth between Mexico City and a provincial town, but the resemblance ends there. In *La Luciérnaga* Azuela admirably fused the actions that take place in different places. The reader is transported directly from the mind of one character in Mexico City to that of another in his home town without the train trip customarily found in previous novels. Most of the action unfolds in the minds of the protagonist, Dionisio, in Mexico City, and of his brother, José María, in the provincial town.

The slender narrative thread deals with the physical and spiritual decay of Dionisio, the provincial, honest man who, with his family, settles in Mexico City. Unlike the Vásquez Prado of *Las tribulaciones,* Dionisio's family was not driven away from the provinces, but went voluntarily to Mexico City, attracted by the promise of a richer life. Soon after arriving, Dionisio and the members of his family discover that they have been deceived. Life in Mexico City is rotten; the inhabitants of the great metropolis live a daily life of trickery, mutual distrust, and general restlessness. Dionisio's inheritance, fifteen thousand pesos, evaporates as if by magic, and he ends up driving a city bus.

In the opening scene of this novel, in which the author vividly describes the collision of Dionisio's bus with a streetcar, the reader is placed inside the character's mind by the simple device of the interior monologue, which Azuela handles with great skill. Dionisio, under the influence of drugs, gives a very personal view of the world, revealing at the same time his warped personality. The same method is used to reveal the character of Dionisio's brother, the miser José María. The chapter dedicated to the analysis of the miser's moral conflict (he blames himself for the damnation of Dionisio and his family) stands out as Azuela's best novelistic effort. The scene of the miser's agony and death, made tense by the use of a chopped style, is reminiscent of some of the somber scenes in Dostoevsky's novels.

The violent nature of the two principal characters, Dionisio and José María, is softened by the presence of Conchita, Dionisio's wife. Unlike the violent brothers, she moves like a shadow, silently tending to her work, always trying to keep the family together. She is characterized as the ideal Mexican wife who obediently follows her husband, whether he is sick, poor, or even tainted by vice or crime. Conchita is like a firefly who carries out her mission by glowing in the dark night, even though her glow may make the night appear darker.

Between *The Tribulations of a Decent Family* and *The Firefly* there is a marked change in the attitude of Azuela toward life in Mexico City. The members of Procopio's family, with the exception of Berta, are able, in spite of social degradation, to redeem their lives and find a new hope in the city's new order. This does not happen in *The Firefly,* for Azuela's disillusionment with the new revolutionary governments has increased. Dionisio finds not only great tribulations in the city but also economic ruin, moral degradation, and spiritual bankruptcy. When he wants to earn a living by investing his money and working honestly, he is thwarted, deceived, robbed, and cast aside by corrupt elements of society. When he joins those elements, opens a *pulquería* (a saloon where *pulque* is sold) and makes money, it is too late. His daughter María Cristina, sixteen years old, has been killed while attending a party given by some unscrupulous politicians, and his son Sebastián dies of tuberculosis, although he is given medical attention. When Conchita goes home to visit her relatives in their home town, his descent is accelerated; he sleeps in the streets and looks for food in the garbage dumps with the skinny and hungry dogs. But there is a limit to his moral degradation; he does not become a criminal, although he is urged by his friends to do so. The novel ends on a note of optimism. Conchita returns to find Dionisio dying in the hospital, but she nurses him back to life and, it is assumed, uplifts him morally.

Besides the protagonists, the reader finds in the pages of *The Firefly* a number of minor characters representative of the underworld as found in Mexico City at the time during which the action takes place. Chirno represents the thief and killer who masquerades as a mild-mannered person, helped by his appearance and especially his angelic face and feminine voice; la Generala, friend of the corrupt politicians, represents the woman-shark, destroyer of men; Benito is the pharmacist without a title who assumes the function of doctor among the poor and ignorant; don Chole the incurable, unemployed member of society, who never tires of repeating: "No one taught me to work, nor did I ever acquire such a ridiculous custom." Then there are also Estrella, Benito's unfaithful mistress, the retired judge Teodomiro, and many others, all descendants of the characters created by Fernández de Lizardi who lived in the same city and in almost identical conditions, although in another era.

The value of this novel, however, lies not only in the painting of these memorable characters. The masterful descriptions of Mexico City's slums have not been equalled by any other contemporary novelist, not even by the famous Carlos Fuentes in his novel *Where the Air Is Clear,* considered one of the best novels about life in the capital. In Azuela's novel there are short realistic descriptions of the *pulquerías,* of the lowest type of *congales,* and of the filthy and crowded streets. His descriptions of the tenement houses are unforgettable:

Conchita, with a heroic resolution, went out to look for her daughter, closing her eyes when she could, but not her ears, which were stubbornly open. She crossed a long corridor, spread out over the muddy floor, an emaciated dog owned by the quarrelsome and evil-spoken woman next door, the sleeping cat, unmindful of his mange and his ticks, the blind little girl sunbathing by the door of her room, the paraplegic man sitting like a king on a shoeshine box among pigeons, chickens and turkey-chicks in search of worms, passing his years seeing, smelling, and cursing. And there she found María Cristina, carrying on a pleasant and friendly chat with the unkempt females of the washing place where monstrous conversations poured forth: everything that can germinate in a primitive mind which has been able to assimilate only the filthiest and most infamous aspects of civilized life.[8]

Also impressive is the description of a street in the slums:

> They cross a street corner where a group of vagrants look at them with suspicion. They jump over a sewer of filthy water where dead cats and dogs can be seen. And no one pays attention to the stupid sign written on a wall: "Wash your hands before you eat." They go through groups of tramps, people who find it so difficult to look at someone straight in the eye, or to say a complete sentence in standard speech. In their grim glances and their drawn lips there are spurts of angry hatred, of contempt, of insolence. It is a world of dogs and dunghills. Dogs of all colors, of all sizes, and of all races. Lean, shriveled-up, bristly. Some lack an ear, others a leg, most have long scars on their backs or on their bellies, the result of the knives that have been tested for sharpness on them. Because there are people who are human, too human.[9]

Thus, on almost any page there are other descriptions, no less impressive, which make this novel stand out in contemporary Mexican fiction. There is no doubt that *The Firefly* is, after *Los de abajo,* Azuela's best novel. About this, all the critics are in agreement.

CHAPTER 5

The Political Novels

I Comrade Pantoja

D ISILLUSIONED with the corrupt public life prevailing in Mexico City, Azuela turned his back to politics and took refuge in the writing of historical novels. But this interlude was to be short-lived. It was difficult for Azuela to close his eyes to political events. In fact, it could be assumed that he kept on writing about contemporary life, for it was in 1937 that he published another novel, *Comrade Pantoja,* the first of a new series dealing with political problems. This novel also marks a new departure in technique. With it Azuela abandons the experimental method used so successfully in *La Malhora* and *The Firefly* to return to the straightforward manner of previous periods. Perhaps the change was dictated by the fact that Azuela wanted to reach a wider reading public than had been reached with the experimental novels.

Equally important with the change in technique is the change of subject matter. Beginning with *Comrade Pantoja,* the most important preoccupation seems to be the unveiling of the many injustices committed by the new rulers and not the creation of a work of art. In these novels, therefore, the artist yields to the man of wrath exposing his country's evils as found in the body politic. He throws discretion to the wind and attacks the corrupt politicians directly, without stopping to think of the consequences.

In the first of the new novels, *El Camarada Pantoja (Comrade Pantoja),* Azuela exposes the politicians who, under the protection of Alvaro Obregón and Plutarco Elías Calles, were making use of their positions to gain personal fortunes. The antihero, Comrade Pantoja, an ignorant factory worker in Mexico City, becomes governor of Zacatecas, although he has no qualifications for the position.

Pantoja's rise in public life is depicted with sarcasm. It so happens that one night General Calderas, a member of the powerful political group Obregón-Calles, is being pursued and takes refuge, by chance, in Pantoja's house. La Chata, Pantoja's wife, hides Calderas and later helps him to escape. As a reward, Catarino Pantoja is given a position at police headquarters. After a short stay in Ciudad Obregón in the company of the political gunman, Lechuga, he becomes a representative in the National Congress. Again rewarded, this time for having killed a political enemy of his bosses, he is made governor of the State of Zacatecas.

In the process of becoming a political success, Pantoja has ruined his private life. Influenced by political associates who have shed their old wives and taken on younger ones, Pantoja decides to get rid of La Chata and takes up with Cecilia, the daughter of Don Benedicto, a respected middle-class merchant. But La Chata does not give in easily, and she kills Cecilia, thus thwarting Pantoja's dream.

The action in *Comrade Pantoja,* like that in *El desquite* and *La Luciérnaga,* takes place in Mexico City and a small town in the interior of the nation. The movement of the protagonist from the city to the town, as in *Las moscas* and *El desquite,* is done by train, and here Azuela takes the opportunity to describe the official train in which President Obregón traveled throughout the country, and also to describe all kinds of political hangers-on, not all of whom, however, are in favor of the government in power or of its policies. In a conversation held between two old revolutionaries, one of the speakers severely criticizes the actions of both Obregón and Calles. To justify this criticism, Azuela has one of the speakers say: "A thorough revolutionary has the right to say whatever he wishes to say" (I, 707). Azuela's attitude toward all revolutionaries has changed completely since the days of *Los de abajo:* "I feel sorry for these poor wretches. When I found them the first time, they captivated me with their candid looks, with their unaffected questions. They were bewildered farmers, workers in rags, miserable tramps or simple beasts of burden. But today these dandies, inflated because their gunman activities have been rewarded and are now salaried gunmen, make me become indignant, and it nauseates me" (I, 707). Not everything, however, has been lost; there is hope of a change for the better: "What is evil in the work of the Revolution is destined to lose; its good aspects, which dominate, will endure for the good of mankind" (I, 707).

It is not in this novel, however, where Azuela presents the good aspects of the revolution. Here everything is bad. Government is controlled by subhuman men; killing the members of the opposition is the only way they know to govern. To hold a position in the government it is necessary to be a killer. As Comrade Pantoja puts it, the successful representative is the one who earns his place in Congress the right way—by using his dagger or his pistol.

Perhaps Azuela was justified in taking an attitude of stern disapproval, as the period he depicts in his novel was one of intense personal struggle to obtain a position in the government. The novel, written in 1928,[1] but not published until 1931, was severely criticized. The author was accused of presenting only one side of the question.[2] Azuela responded with calm and common sense. Among other things, he said: "Some critics have said that in my novels of the Revolution I have expressed half the truth, and this is perhaps the greatest praise I could have received. But I do not accept it because it is not true. Truth has a thousand faces, and a man can only give reality to that aspect of the truth he has in front of him. It is not half the truth that I have given, but only a very small part of it, my truth, which I have presented with honesty and fidelity." [3]

The novel may reflect the truth as Azuela saw it, but as a work of art it is inferior to his other works. His overzealous interest in exposing political misdeeds makes him careless with characterization, structure, description, and plot development. In the whole novel there cannot be found a single character, with the possible exception of a minor one, La Chata, worthy of Azuela. Besides, the characters move in a world that is oversimplified and therefore false. Thus, the novel has value only as a social document about a period in Mexican history that is known for its political instability and corruption, a period of transition between the violent event of the revolution and the establishment of a stable and responsible government. It is significant that Azuela, in the second edition of the novel, made several changes with the purpose of softening the previous accusations. In 1951 he wrote: "Last year I had to rewrite it partially for a second edition, and I do not know if it is better or worse than the first. No other novel has given me so much trouble as this one, nor have I ever been so dissatisfied with a work of mine" (III, 1101–2).

II San Gabriel de Valdivias, comunidad indígena

The title of this novel, published in 1938, would be more appropriate for a sociological or anthropological study of a rural community; but in spite of its poor title, the novel has merit. The descriptions of rural life are the best written by Azuela since his early novels. He forgets here for a moment life in Mexico City and concentrates on depicting a rural community in which the farmers are still struggling, in spite of the revolution and its rural reforms, to keep their land from falling into the hands of the new *caciques,* the unscrupulous revolutionaries eager to take advantage of the new social situation. In this sense, this novel is similar to that of Mauricio Magdaleno, *El resplandor (Sunburst),* published in 1937.

When the large hacienda of the Valdivias family, San Gabriel, is subdivided and distributed among the farmers, the political leader, Saturnino Quintana, takes advantage of the situation to take possession of the land. To keep the farmers happy, he has a road and a dam built. This does not fool the farmers, and soon they revolt against the new master, the *cacique.* The opposition centers around Ciriaco Campos, a young man who has returned to settle in the *comunidad* after having been in the army fighting against Huerta and the *federales.* The clash between Saturnino and Ciriaco is unavoidable. In the first encounter Ciriaco has the upper hand, but is forced to take refuge in the mountains. Saturnino, with the help of some gunmen, takes revenge on Juanita, Ciriaco's sweetheart. Saturnino is finally defeated and killed, but not before he has almost exterminated the whole *comunidad.* Azuela's pessimistic attitude is reflected in the final outcome when Major Pérez, who is worse than Saturnino, arrives to take over the administration of the community. The author's message is expressed by the local teacher, Ramoncito, who keeps on repeating: "My brothers, we got rid of the *hacendados,* now let's get rid of the political bosses!" (I, 783).

The farmers in this novel are well characterized. Azuela knew firsthand the mentality of Mexico's rural inhabitants, and when he portrays them, he never hesitates. In this novel there are also several very well-drawn dramatic scenes, especially those in which the farmers and the political bosses from the city clash. Azuela's sympathy is always on the side of rural Mexico. As in his novels of the revolution, he also takes delight here in painting the landscape and associating its moods to those of the characters. It is this element that makes San Gabriel de Valdivias superior to the novels of the city.

III Regina Landa

In Regina Landa, published in 1939, Azuela returns to Mexico City, this time to depict the life of a girl typical of thousands working for the federal government. Regina, daughter of an honest revolutionary general, is left alone and without means of support on the death of her father when she is twenty. An old friend of the family, the bureaucrat Sánchez, is able to get a job for Regina as a typist in the office of one of the ministers. Soon Regina discovers how sordid the life of the clerk is, since all they care about is to hold their jobs, regardless of the ideas of the politicians in power. Their motto is: "First eat and then think." After working as secretary to the minister and discovering the secrets of his office, Regina gains her independence and establishes a business of her own.

From the point of view of plot development, Regina Landa is one of Azuela's poorest novels. Less than a plot, Regina's adventures as a working girl are nothing but a thinly disguised excuse to criticize bureaucratic life during the government of President Lázaro Cárdenas. Azuela's theory seems to be that the state prostitutes its employees because it forces them to breathe the air of the most abject and servile submission. The characters found in this novel are simple examples of the corrupt type of employee that works for the government. All of them behave like castrated souls who, in order to eat poorly, humble themselves at the feet of their masters, as they live under the terror of being fired. In this novel Azuela seems to have lost all sense of proportion, as his criticism is extended to intellectuals, artists, and everyone that has received financial help from the government.

Azuela's desire to moralize, which was the result of his indignation, made him forget that he was writing a work of art and result is an illogical story. This novel, indeed, reflects Azuela's not a political denunciation. And it is precisely this lack of control, this lack of proportion, that weakens his argument, for the abhorrence of anything that had to do with the government workers. It is for these reasons that *Regina Landa* must be classified as one of Azuela's weakest novels.

IV Avanzada

In *Regina Landa,* Azuela's ire falls upon the bureaucrats; in *Avanzada,* he flagellates labor leaders and agrarian reformists. Published in 1940, the last year of Cárdenas' period in office, the novel treats of contemporary events and criticizes the president's agrarian policies. The action takes place first in the old hacienda of Don Miguel, whose death is the result of the government's action in taking possession of his land. His son Adolfo, who has studied agriculture in the United States and Canada, is thwarted by the *agraristas* when he tries to introduce new methods of cultivating the land. When the government takes over his last plot of land, he migrates to the State of Veracruz and goes to work in a sugar mill.

In the second part of the novel, the conflict is not between the *hacendados* and *agraristas* but between the workers and the labor leaders. Just as he had fought against the *agraristas* in Jalisco, Adolfo, with the help of his friend Torres, fights the corrupt labor leaders in Veracruz. Their opposition to the new masters of the people is paid for dearly, as they both lose their lives in the struggle.

Avanzada, with its change of locale from Jalisco to Veracruz, loses its unity and, except for the presence of Adolfo, could be considered as two novels in one. But even the hero, Adolfo, is a different person in the second part. As a farmer, his only ambition is to make money; in the second part, he has become a missionary whose only motivation is to help the oppressed. An unaccounted-for change also takes place in Margarita, the other character that appears in both parts. First, as Adolfo's sweetheart, she is just a simple farm girl; in the second part, as Adolfo's wife, she is characterized as possessing a strong character (*"un carácter granítico"*).

In spite of the lack of unity, *Avanzada* is less artificial than *El Camarada Pantoja* or *Regina Landa.* There are some well-drawn scenes, especially those that take place in the hacienda, in the first part. It is, at the same time, less pessimistic than other novels of this period. The novel ends with an optimistic note: when

Adolfo dies, his son is born. Adolfo and Margarita, despite all adversities, work toward a better world, in which they must have faith. Evil and corruption can, after all, be conquered. "Christian culture, which is based on love, files the claws of this new tiger, neutralizes the poison of this new serpent and reduces the criminal to a harmless being, and often converts him into a person useful to society" (I, 1099).

V Nueva burguesía

In *Nueva burguesía,* published in 1941, Azuela continues the attack against the government of Lázaro Cárdenas. The action takes place in 1939, when Avila Camacho and Almazán were campaigning for the presidency. Azuela criticizes the methods used by the political party in power to elect the new president. This theme, however, is hardly developed. The importance of this novel lies in the descriptions of the new social classes that have appeared, as the author observes them in a tenement house in the neighborhood of Nonoalco, not far from where he himself lived. There is an endless procession of characters which makes this novel a true human comedy. There is Bartolo, the poor but happy shoemaker; Rosita, the unfaithful wife; the bus driver Chabelón and his insane mother; the sisters Escamilla, servants turned into office girls; the old maid Emmita in search of a husband; Miguelito, Campillo; and many others.

Azuela's technique in *Nueva burguesía* is cinematographic. He rapidly passes from scene to scene, giving closeups of his characters, without worrying too much about transition between scenes. No single action is important, except, perhaps, the killing of the linotypist Benavides, but all of them together carry an impact superior to that of many novels structured around a single action. No less important is the nature of the dialogues, always interesting and adapted to the social status of the characters. Azuela knew tenement life in Mexico City well and could depict it better than a trained sociologist, as can well be seen in this rather short novel, perhaps the best of this period.

VI La marchanta

Azuela published no novels during 1942 and 1943. During these years he became interested in the American novel, and expecially in John Dos Passos. The influence of the latter's *Man-*

hattan Transfer, which Azuela read in 1941, is evident in *La marchanta,* a novel about life in Mexico City published in 1944. Compared with his previous novels, there is a noticeable absence of attacks against the government and the people's oppressors. His main preoccupation seems to be the drawing of characters who are the victims of their own weaknesses and not of social forces. The story is told from the point of view of the protagonists, and the chapters are named after them: Juan Cocoliso (also named Santiago), Fernanda, La Marchanta (a woman street vender). The name "marchanta" is generic: it is applied to Fernanda's mother, to Fernanda herself, and to her ancestors on her mother's side. The novel ends with Fernanda selling in the same street booth that had belonged to her mother.

The central theme is the influence that money suddenly acquired has upon the personality of a poor city dweller. Juan Cocoliso, a poor boy, marries the Marchanta's daughter, although he does not love her. He works for Don Cosme, whose grocery store he inherits. The store is not worth much, but hidden in one of the walls Juan finds Don Cosme's life savings. The change that takes place in Juan's personality is complete. He stops working and lets his wife take care of the store; he takes up with the café singer Linda Palma and abandons his wife and business. The end is disastrous: he drinks himself to death. This is not the case with his wife, Fernanda, who does not give up her store in spite of the money. Her behavior, in a sense, contradicts Azuela's thesis about the corrupting power of money. This inconsistency weakens the central idea of the novel, and the message does not come through very clearly.

VII La mujer domada

In *La mujer domada (The Tamed Woman),* a novel published in 1946, Serafina, unlike Fernanda, has great ambitions and is able to rise from her humble origins and attend the Law School of the University of Mexico. But her defeat is no less real. After undergoing a great many indignities, she is forced to give up her studies and return to Morelia, her home town, where she marries a storekeeper whom she had rejected previously.

Although this novel does not add to what the author had said in *La Luciérnaga* and *Regina Landa,* it presents an excellent description of life in Morelia, in the State of Michoacán, where part

of the novel takes place, and a good picture of how students live
in Mexico City, but not of university life, which Azuela knew
only through his experiences in Guadalajara as a young man. He
contrasts always life in the city and life in the small town, praising
the latter and speaking with scorn of the former. Mexico City, the
tamer of Serafina, attracts young students from the provinces not
to educate them but to destroy them. "Is it worthwhile," Serafina
asks herself, "to go through it all again only to obtain a sheepskin
worth less than the paper on which it is written and which au-
thorizes you to keep on dying of hunger?" (II, 347). It must be
pointed out, however, that Serafina's failure is not due to the
inefficiencies of the capital's social organization, but to her own
inability. Before leaving her home town, Serafina had no appreciation of its way of life. It took years of suffering in Mexico City
to awaken her to its values. When she returns to Morelia, she is
for the first time conscious of its wholesome atmosphere. "She
delights in breathing the pure air; she cannot hear enough, smell
enough. Now she feels she is among her own, in the place she
should never have abandoned. In the Capital she never had a
single moment of similar satisfaction. She always felt like a
stranger, like an intruder" (II, 334–35).

Azuela's purpose in this novel is too obvious. He wants the
girls to remain at home and not be dazzled by the attractions of
the capital, or by the prestige of its university. Was he justified in
trying to keep the young men and women, even the bright ones,
in the provinces? Whether he was or not, he was sincere in be-
lieving that city life corrupts, that it is better to remain at home
and save your soul than to sacrifice it for a trained mind in the new
Babel.

VIII Sendas perdidas

Sendas perdidas (*Lost Paths*) is the last novel that Azuela published during his lifetime. It was first written as a script for a
movie that was never produced. The script was later enlarged and
published as a novel in 1949. The plot, which deals with the
man-eating woman, is not very original even for Azuela, as it is
found in *La Marchanta,* although not developed there.

Gregorio, an efficient, honest and generous worker, ruins his
life trying to convert Lucero, a beautiful nightclub singer without
moral principles. He may have an ulterior motive, since Lucero is

the mistress of Gustavo, his half brother. The novel has a semi-tragic ending, as Gregorio kills his half brother and wounds Lucero, who continues living as before. Not so Gregorio, who recovers his lost path after he is forgiven by a lenient judge.
There is nothing new in this novel, either in plot or technique. Azuela repeats himself. Gregorio and Lucero are projections of Juan Cocoliso and Linda Palma, characters who appear in *La Marchanta*. A departure from Azuela's choice of events makes *Sendas perdidas* the only novel in which he dramatizes events of the past. The year after he published the novel, he made this observation: *"Sendas perdidas* was composed with characters and events of more than fifty years ago, when I first began to practice my profession" (III, 1044). Was this novel written, or perhaps outlined, in 1900? The naturalistic attitude of the author in the novel points in that direction. If this is so, it would be consistent with Azuela's technique of dramatizing only contemporary events, except for his historical novels.

CHAPTER 6

The Posthumous Novels

I La maldicion *and* Esa sangre

A ZUELA did not publish any novels during the last three years of his life. He did, however, write at least two, published posthumously: *La maldición* in 1955 and *Esa sangre* in 1956.[1]

In *La maldición* (*The Curse*) Azuela repeats his favorite theme: the destruction of the family from rural Mexico who decides to migrate to the capital. Upon the death of the farmer, Basilio Montelongo, who has been divested of his land by the government, his family—Emilia, Rodulfo, and Magdalena—leave the farm and go to Mexico City. On the way they stop at Celaya to say goodbye to an uncle, who tells them: "Here in Celaya you could live modestly working like honest people. . . . But no, what you are looking for is something else. I do not know if you can become rich in Mexico City, but what I can tell you is that the happiness and tranquillity you have left in your souls will be lost there" (II, 468). Emilia, the mother, considers the uncle's pronouncement to be a curse upon the family.

In the capital *"la maldición"* is fulfilled. Rodulfo has to work as a street cleaner and his mother and sister as doorkeepers in a tenement house. Rodulfo, although a farmer, turns out to be as tricky and cunning as the city dwellers and soon becomes rich by illicit means. Having lost his moral scruples, he makes a prostitute of his sister. Five years later both Rodulfo and his sister Magdalena are physical and moral ruins; the uncle's curse is thus fulfilled.

Why didn't Azuela publish this novel? Perhaps he did not think it was ready to be published. The novel has several defects, especially in its structure. The first part unfolds on the farm of "Las Maravillas" and in the city of Celaya. From there the reader is taken to Mexico City with the Montelongo family. In the capital the mother finally gives up struggling against unsurmountable difficulties and returns to Celaya, at which point Azuela writes about the life of Uncle Carlos, a minor character. The novelist here has abandoned the principal characters in Mexico City, and in order to bring the reader up to the present, he introduces five letters from Magdalena to her mother telling about her experiences and those of Rodulfo. It seems that Azuela, tired of the story, tried to abbreviate it by giving the reader a résumé of the events in Mexico City. Here the novel could have ended. However, the novelist brings the reader back to Mexico City, where he dramatizes the events already known, and again delights in painting the corruption prevalent in the government, this time under President Alemán. The basic moral principle of these bureaucrats seems to be: "Fraud is never punished." The moral lesson that Azuela wants to communicate is found in one of Rodulfo's thoughts, which he never puts into practice: "For the first time in his life he thought that he also could become adjusted to this limited, humble happiness with which thousands of human beings are satisfied: a modest home, an unexhausting job, and peace at heart" (II, 592–93). However, the novel's thesis—the damnation of the people who go to Mexico City from the provinces—is unacceptable. In spite of the tragic nature of this theme, there are several humorous scenes in this otherwise insignificant novel.

Esa sangre (Blood Tells), published in 1956, is a continuation of an earlier novel, *Mala yerba* (1909). Here Azuela returns to the theme of the struggle between the farmers and the *peones,* although his interest has shifted from the description of the physical struggle to the psychological problems faced by some of the characters, especially the protagonist, Julián Andrade, now a poor, feeble old man who has given up his lordly manners.

By picking up the story of the characters introduced in *Mala yerba* Azuela has the opportunity of comparing the Mexico of Don Porfirio and that of Lázaro Cárdenas. He leaves with the reader the impression that he favors the world he so much detested during his early years. The locale where the events of *Esa sangre* take place, however, is not exactly the same as that of the earlier novel. The hacienda of the Andrade family, now in ruins, is the locale of only one short scene, a sentimental trip that the old man Andrade takes to see what is left of his old hunting grounds. Most of the action in this last novel takes place in the small town of San Francisquito, now inhabited by numerous outsiders who do not know who the Andrades are or were. The

mayor is Gertrudis, a nephew of Julián Andrade's old rival.
Among the new characters there is *El Fruncido,* the representative
of the National Agrarian Commission and the villain in the novel.
He is characterized as "insolent, vulgar, and brutal." He is the
new master of the town, and not even a native of the region,
since he was sent by the central government. The local people
soon discover that he was "as much a thief as he was a killer"
(II, 669).

In spite of the odds against him, Azuela is able to reconstruct
the life of Andrade, from the time that he joined Villa's forces
until he returns to Mexico City from South and Central America.
Most of the novel deals with Andrade's struggle against the
government for the purpose of recovering his old possessions, now
in the hands of the *peones.* What turns out to be the most interesting part of the novel is Andrade's struggle with himself to control
his fiery blood. He is unable to recover his land or to conquer
himself and dies fighting a Western-style duel with *El Fruncido.*
Azuela reconstructs Andrade's life by means of the flashback
without disrupting the novel's unity. Andrade, of course, remi-
nisces about his life on the hacienda, and several of the scenes of
Mala yerba are mentioned. For the reader unacquainted with the
earlier novel, there is a résumé of the plot. Although Azuela is
not able to improve upon the scenes of *Mala yerba,* in the psychological analysis of the protagonist, he surpasses his former effort.

CHAPTER 7

Minor Works

I *The Short Stories*

ALTHOUGH Azuela began his writing with short stories, he gave up the short narrative as soon as he had published his first novel. Now and then, however, a short story bearing his name would appear in the newspapers and periodicals of Mexico City or Guadalajara. The short stories published between 1896 and 1900 are written in a style reminiscent of his novels where the naturalistic elements predominate. The most interesting of his first *impresiones* (he does not call them *cuentos* [short stories]), are "De mi tierra" ("From My Native Land"), which won a prize in the literary contest held in Lagos de Moreno in 1903, and "Esbozo," "Víctimas de la opulencia," "En derrota," and "Avichuelos negros" ("Black Birds"). The principal character in "Esbozo" is a medical student whose mental capacity is much below that required to undertake the study of this difficult subject. Of interest in this story is the characterization of the student, where the tendency to exaggerate certain traits is employed with effectiveness. In "De mi tierra," social criticism and satire predominate. The servant Teodora cunningly explains to her husband Macedonio why their son has blond hair like that of the landowner. In "Víctimas de la opulencia," published in 1904, Azuela for the first time uses a theme that he is to exploit in all his later works: the injustices committed by the rich against the poor. In the next story, "En derrota," the tragedy is the result of the preponderant advantages that the overseer's son has over the peon in their rivalry for the love of Camila. "Avichuelos negros" is perhaps the best rounded-out story of this early period. The title, "The Black Birds," refers to the townswomen who watch over the morals of the inhabitants. María's lover is dying, and these "good women" will not let her be with him. The lover dies unattended, and rats gnaw his feet. Criticism of the small-town meddler is thus very well dramatized. Azuela was long ago recognized as the creator of the novel of the revolution. Not so well known is the fact that it was he who also wrote the first short stories about the revolution. The first story about this struggle was "De cómo al fin lloró Juan Pablo" ("How Juan Pablo Finally Cried"), first published in New York in the *Revista Universal,* June 15, 1918.[1] Another of his short stories, "El caso López Romero," was written even earlier, in April 1916, although it was not published until after his death.[2] There is no doubt that this story was written in 1916, as is evident by the following quotation, also found in *Los de abajo.* López Romero is the same character who in *The Underdogs* appears under the name of Valderrama. López Romero, like Valderrama, says:

Villa? . . . Carranza? . . . Obregon? . . . X . . . Y . . . Z . . . Doctor, I love the revolution like I love an erupting volcano. I love the volcano because it is a volcano, and the revolution because it is a revolution. As to the stones left underneath or on top, what do I care about them?[3]

López Romero, like Valderrama and José María in another story about the revolution,[4] reflects aspects of the character of a personal friend of Azuela, the lawyer José Becerra. The tragic ending of another good friend, General Leocadio Parra, who fought under the orders of General Medina, gave Azuela the idea for "De cómo al fin lloró Juan Pablo," perhaps his best short story.

The above are fictionalized events in the lives of friends. In other stories about the revolution, the characters cannot be identified, and the themes are more general. In the story, "Y ultimadamente," Azuela narrates the unnecessary death of a musician who happens to have a room in a hotel where there are no vacancies. The Colonel needs a room for that night, and the musician is the victim. The technique used by Azuela in this story is that of the dialogue, in which, like a telephone conversation, only one of the speakers is heard. In this case the reader is made aware of the situation through the conversation of the Colonel who speaks to the woman who runs the hotel, while she remains behind closed doors.

In a few of his stories Azuela forgets about the character to emphasize the anecdote. In the story "La nostalgia de mi coronel" (1937), the character serves only to dramatize a case of sadism. The Colonel feels nostalgia for the days when, in active service, he could rid himself of his bad humor by whipping the first person that came across his path. In some of his other stories the purpose, as in his political novels, is to criticize those who made use of the revolution to become rich; this is the theme of the stories "Anuncios a línea desplegada" (1937) and "Un rebelde," the latter published in Spain in 1929.

There are still other stories written by Azuela that do not treat of the revolution. "El jurado" ("The Jury") seems to be a page taken from his novel *La Malhora*. "Era un hombre honrado" ("He Was an Honorable Man") is a psychological study of the person whose character is based on fraud.

In general it could be said that Azuela's stories are more like scenes not used in his many novels. For this reason they are often not well rounded. His technique is that of a novelist and not that of a short story writer, and he was seldom successful with the short narrative.[5]

II *The Three Dramas*

Mariano Azuela was not a dramatist. His interest in the theater, however, was deep-seated. From his student days in Guadalajara until his death in 1952, he never stopped being interested in the theater and in the movies. His three dramas are original, but dramatized, versions of three of his novels: *Los de abajo, El buho en la noche* (*El desquite*), and *Del Llano Hermanos, S. en C.* (*Los caciques*). Compared to the novels from which they are taken, the dramas lack the spark of life that characterizes his fiction. Azuela himself recognized this fact. He wrote: "The harsh truth is that the novelist (as a dramatist) forgets a fundamental fact: he is not offering the public a novel but a drama or a script, which differs radically from the novel, from which they have taken only the framework for a new structure. A beautiful description requires many pages from the writer and many minutes of attention from the part of the reader, while on the stage or on the screen, it goes by like a flash" (O.C., III, 1149).

As a drama, *The Underdogs* is reduced to six unrelated scenes. Although it was successful both as a drama and as a movie, it lacks the force that is found in the novel. On the other hand, the drama *El buho en la noche* helps to interpret the novel *El desquite* from which it is taken. But even here, as in the third drama, *Del Llano Hermanos, S. en C.*, the depth in characterization found in the novels is missing. During the last years of his life Azuela prepared a dramatized version of his biography, *Pedro Moreno, el Insurgente*. This version, however, has never been published in book form. Unpublished until after his death is also the script he prepared for a movie based on the life of Madero.[6]

III *The Four Biographies*

In his first fictionalized biography, *Pedro Moreno, el Insurgente* (1933), Azuela re-creates a historical event which took place in his native state during the period of the Wars of Independence. It is a well-known episode; the heroic defense of Fuerte del Sombrero by Pedro Moreno, a native of the state of Jalisco, and the Spanish General Francisco Xavier Mina. The book is dedicated to the memory of Father Agustín Rivera, whose vivid account of the episode inspired Azuela to write his biography of Moreno.

More than a historical novel, this book by Azuela could be classified as an *episodio nacional* after the form used in Spain by Galdós and in Mexico by Olavarría y Ferrari, Salado Alvarez, and others. The most interesting parts of the book are the descriptions of the defense of the fort by Moreno and his followers, the portrait of the heroic Spanish general, and the disagreement between the officers of both leaders. Unfortunately, Azuela abandons his heroes (chapters 8 to 11) to talk about secondary and unimportant aspects of the battle. The action, as is to be expected, is seen from the point of view of the defenders. This does not preclude the presentation of the other side, which is done by means of letters. Although the author has presented a colorful picture and has been able to re-create the historical event, the book lacks the force and realism characteristic of his work, especially the novels of the revolution.

For his second biographical work, *Precursores* (1935), Azuela relates the lives of three famous outlaws: El Amito, Manuel Lozada, and Antonio Rojas. The three are considered by Azuela, in a satirical manner, to be precursors of the men of the revolution. The first, El Amito, was a famous outlaw in the region called El Bajío, in central Mexico. The second, Manuel Lozada, also called "El Tigre de Alica," kept the government busy in his native region of Nayarit for many years. In these two fictionalized biographies Azuela is unable to add anything new or important to what had already been written about these men. In the third biography, called *El hombre masa,* he writes about the deeds of the *guerrillero,* Antonio Rojas. Here Azuela abandons the straightforward retelling in third person by the author and lets a *compadre* of Rojas, Teodosio Laris, tell the reader about the hero. By this means, Azuela is able to penetrate the mind of Rojas, and the result is a vivid, realistic story, much superior to the previous two. The novelist, as is often the case, triumphs over the historian.

The next biography written was that of Father Agustín Rivera, the most significant representative of Lagos de Moreno prior to the appearance of Azuela. The book, *El Padre don Agustín Rivera* (1942), was not the first account of the life of the sage of Lagos written by Azuela. In 1912 he had already published a note on this remarkable man in the *Revista Blanca* of Guadalajara. Since then he had never lost interest in writing a book on Rivera. But in spite of Azuela's admiration and even reverence for this man, his book does not represent his best effort; it is uninteresting and contains many errors, as was pointed out by the critic Francisco González León.[7]

Azuela left unpublished a fictionalized biography of Francisco I. Madero. It appeared for the first time in 1960 in the third volume of his complete works. It is not known if Azuela wrote this work before or after his biography of Pedro Moreno, but he does use the same technique of mixing history and fiction. The work was first prepared to serve as a script for a motion picture. The editor, Alí Chumacero, found in Azuela's library several versions, only one of which was in final form; it had been turned into the form of a novel based on the life of Madero. Azuela himself never mentions this work in his autobiography.

The book, divided into four chapters, opens with a scene in the National Palace where President Porfirio Díaz is entertaining his friends with a gala dance. There the reader meets a young man, Manuel Figueroa, an ardent follower of Madero, and the widow, Virginia Martínez, daughter of General Martínez. The widow saves Figueroa's life by misleading some agents of Díaz who know about Figueroa's intentions. It is Manuel who tells Virginia about Madero and his activities before his imprisonment in San Luis

Potosí. Together they are able to escape the vigilance of Díaz'
agents and join Madero in that town. From here on the author
tells the story in third person: Madero's return from the United
States, where he had taken refuge, the deeds of Villa and Orozco,
and the final triumph of the revolution. In the final chapter the
reader travels with Madero to Mexico City, is informed about
Zapata's uprising, the counterrevolution against Madero, and
finally the death of the hero. The end of the novel, much more
appropriate for a motion picture than for a novel, is over-
dramatized. Indeed, throughout the work dramatic elements predominate over historical facts. Azuela fails to give the reader a
good picture of Madero, since he is much more interested in
depicting action. His personality is drowned in a sea of unnecessary scenes in which intrigue is paramount.

IV *Literary Criticism*

As a critic, Azuela is best known for his book *Cien años de
novela mexicana* (*The Mexican Novel through a Hundred Years*),
1947, in which he collected the lectures he gave at the Colegio
Nacional in 1943 and 1947. In this work Azuela studies the
novels of Lizardi, Inclán, Altamirano, Delgado, Riva Palacio,
López Portillo y Rojas, Rabasa, San Juan, Gamboa, and Frías.
Less known are his "Divagaciones literarias" (O.C., III, 712–72),
his "Letras de provincia" (O.C., III, 773-811), and his "Grandes
novelistas" (O.C., III, 812–1011). In the first he discusses the
works of his favorite Mexican authors, who seem to be Prieto,
Nájera, Nervo, Micrós, González Obregón, and Maillefert. In
the second he presents portraits of writers born or identified with
his native town, Lagos de Moreno; he talks about Father Rivera,
Alvarez del Castillo, González León, Rafael de Alba, Moreno y
Oviedo, José Becerra, Dr. Reina, and Martínez Valadez. In the
last one he studies extensively the novels of Balzac, Zola, Proust,
and Galdós.

More than literary criticism, these essays by Azuela could be
considered as comments on books and writers. In everything he
read he always looked for the human aspect. It is for this reason
that he considered Sainte-Beuve as the best literary critic who ever
lived. It is this same French critic who influenced Azuela's belief
that the critic should take the position of the average reader who

expresses his opinion without worrying about what others say or have said about the work.

Azuela's basic tenet in his criticism of the novel, and especially of the Mexican novel, is to judge its value according to its acceptance by the general public. For him the novel is an art form of the masses; its structure and its style, therefore, should be of secondary importance to the writer, who should above all be able to tell a story directly and with interest. He admired novels like Inclán's *Astucia,* written "for the people and by the people" (III, 593). On the other hand, he firmly rejected the novel as propaganda or moral doctrine. "Paul Bourget and Emile Zola," he wrote, "lost all their forcefulness as soon as they became social reformers" (III, 611). Azuela insisted that the novel should not be didactic; it should be read for enjoyment, not to obtain information or gain knowledge. It is for this reason that Azuela rejected Altamirano's concept of the novel as a means to educate the masses. But Azuela recognized that in order for a novel to endure, it must be more than just entertaining; it must have other qualities. "The value of a play, a drama, or a novel," he wrote, "depends on its literary features; but if it lacks a solid structure, if its characters are lifeless, if the actions are unbelievable, if the theme lacks human interest, if the problems it presents do not elicit a strong reaction, the work is a failure" (II, 623).

Another important principle of literary criticism according to Azuela, is sincerity. The novelist should strive not to falsify the characters. This is why Azuela strongly criticized the novels of López Portillo y Rojas, whose characters he considered weak because they were copies of those portrayed by Spanish novelists.

Azuela also makes a distinction between what he calls novel and literature. According to him, the principle preoccupation of the Mexican novelist should be to write novels without trying to make literature. He wrote: "What has done the most harm to the novel has been the snobbish attitude of those writers who concentrate on making literature instead of writing novels. If the writer is a man of great capacity to produce because of his natural genius or an exceptional, acquired culture, he should, and ought to, write works of universal value; but we, the modest writers, should devote our writing to what is ours. The fundamental thing is to keep the balance between what we want to do and what we actually do. When I say modest writers, I am referring to those of limited capabilities, to those who do not aspire to be geniuses." [8]

Azuela will undoubtedly be remembered as a novelist and not
as a critic; however, as a novelist he is a shrewd student of the
psychology of the Mexican people; as a man who knew his
country and as a sincere critic, his observations are indispensable
to the student of the Mexican novel.

V *His Autobiography*

In 1949 Azuela began to take seriously the writing of his autobiography, which he had begun years before. Unfortunately this
work, to be called "Autobiografía del otro," was never completed.
Part of it was published under the title *El novelista y su ambiente*
and part under the original title. After the actual writing was
begun, Azuela had doubts about the propriety of writing an autobiography. He said, "Since I conceived the idea of publishing
these chapters, I was struck by the fear and the scruple of seeming
to be presumptuous and vain. To write about oneself is very
serious, if not intolerable" (III, 1193). Azuela's high sense of
honesty and sincerity deprived the student of his autobiography,
except for incomplete aspects of it which are extremely useful in
understanding the man and his work.

Under the title "Autobiografía del otro" he included the *Pre-
liminares,* apparently written in 1938. Even in his autobiography
Azuela makes use of a fictitious character. An imaginary person,
"el otro," in reality his *alter ego,* asks him to write his autobiography, and he says: "I have already reached the age of seventy-
five. The idea had already occurred to me, but I gave it up for
two reasons: first of all, vanity, because an unimportant life is
only recorded by the very vain or the very old; in the second
place, if what I have to say has no interest to me, it will have
less for others" (III, 1178). Perhaps for these reasons Azuela
gave up for awhile the writing of autobiography. It was later
continued, but in a straightforward manner. In *El novelista y
su ambiente,* he no longer tells his life story to the imaginary
person, to the *"otro,"* but directly to the reader. More than an
autobiography, the first part of this work is a disquisition about
his novelistic art. In the second part he continues with exposition
but gives more information about himself. Characteristic of this
autobiography is the fact that Azuela does not follow a chronological order, and it is therefore difficult to piece together the
sequence of events. Nevertheless, it is very useful in the writing of
his biography and in the interpretation of his works.

CHAPTER 8

The Novelist's Craft

I *Setting the Stage*

A ZUELA, fortunately, left in his writings random notes about the techniques he followed in the composition of his novels. He confessed that generally the process began with the creation of the background. He wrote:

> I have a vague idea of what I want to write about: the countryside, the village, the small town; an event that has left an impression in my memory; persons with whom I have sympathized or clashed, etc. With that confused idea in my mind I take pencil and paper in hand or sit at the typewriter and without further ado I begin to scribble or pound the keys without a definite plan. The words come out in a disorganized manner, trampling upon each other, repeating themselves. I know nothing about the characters, events, or definite background. In this diffused form it is perhaps the environment which is the first thing that becomes clear and imperative in my imagination. That is, the necessary background for the characters to be born, grow, reproduce, and die. (III, 1042–43)

In spite of what he says, it is obvious that in the selection of the background Azuela was consciously guided by personal likes and dislikes and by previous experiences. As a rule he selected the world around him as it existed at the time he wrote. In his first novels he re-creates the world he knew: Guadalajara, Lagos de Moreno, the hacienda with its feudal organization. In *María Luisa*, written in Guadalajara, he painted that city's streets, boarding houses, parks, and hospitals. "In the Alameda," he says, "I found the necessary atmosphere and human elements for my novel. In the Alameda, near the wall fence, in the field of tall grass, in the many nooks . . . I saw the beginning or ending of many an idyll. . . . And only a block and a half from the Alameda and four from the hospital was the boarding house of Calle Belén, managed by Doña Cuca and her cousin Juana and where the students lived" (III, 1018, 1025).

After finishing his medical studies and going to Lagos to practice his profession, Azuela forgot Guadalajara and wrote instead about his home town. The background he used in *Los fracasados, Sin amor,* and *Los caciques* is that of Lagos, where these novels were written. About the composition of the first he wrote:

Los fracasados, for many reasons, could appear as a simple report: plot, characters, and background came to me without great effort. My purpose was to concentrate on one aspect and a moment of the life of a town of twelve thousand inhabitants. . . . I visited old streets in dusty neighborhoods; I saw their houses with the plaster peeling off, the sidewalks full of holes, the wall fences marked by large scars. I heard the sound of the hammer on the anvil . . . the ax cutting the meat over the mesquite counter at the butcher shop on Estación Street. . . . (II, 1044, 1047)

And thus he continued with the description of his native town, which served him so well as background for his early novels. Not everything, however, is taken directly from reality. For his next novel, *Sin amor,* instead of looking at his surroundings for background, he copied from a third-rate novelist. The result is an inferior work, as was pointed out earlier. Why did he do it? It is difficult to understand, for he had said: "I love living things, without the adornments dictated by the latest fashions; I love life as it is, with its thousand luminous and colorful aspects. Therefore, *Sin amor* represents something strange in my way of life, something which clashes with my spontaneous and rude frankness and which makes me reject it. . . . My purpose had been to create the dullness and boredom characteristic of a small town so described by Santiago Rusiñol in *El pueblo gris*" (III, 1064). From this failure Azuela learned a lesson: never to let himself be overawed by the technique or the style of another novelist.

In *Mala yerba,* his next novel, he turned away from books to portray the environment he knew so well, the countryside of his native state of Jalisco, especially that of his father's ranch. He wrote: "When I read a description of the sea done with love and veneration, I think that to enjoy it thoroughly it is necessary to have been born and reared near the sea. The same thing happens, I believe, when rural life and the countryside are painted; if it is not absolutely necessary to have been born on a ranch, one must at least be thoroughly acquainted with its nature" (III, 1056).

It is due precisely to this fact that life in *Mala yerba* and again in *Los de abajo* appears so real. Azuela did not like to describe anything he had not seen.

In *Los de abajo,* as in other novels of the revolution, Azuela was able to describe accurately and forcefully a chaotic society, providing the reader with excellent descriptions of the battles, the plundering of towns, and the ravaging of the countryside that went on during those terrible years. In *Las tribulaciones . . .* he depicted the effects of the revolution on the inhabitants of Mexico City. Having settled in the capital, Azuela described his impressions of the society he encountered there in the years immediately following the struggle in novels such as *La Malhora.* Later he wrote of the years of social readjustment, the struggle for power among the triumphant men of the revolution, and the changes brought about by the armed conflicts in such novels as *La Luciérnaga, Regina Landa, Nueva burguesía, La Marchanta, La mujer domada,* and *Sendas perdidas.* In all of them he gives emphasis to the life in the slums.

This technique of depicting immediate surroundings could not be used when he decided to write historical novels. He solved the problem in the case of *Pedro Moreno, el insurgente* by visiting the place where the historical events had taken place. About the composition of this work he tells the reader: "After I had enough information about the historical events, I observed, when I began to write, that I lacked something, something that I could not find in any written book or document: the scenery of the place where the events had taken place. Although my writings have been of pure imagination, I have based them on events I have witnessed or which have been related to me by reliable and trustworthy persons. It is easier for me to reconstruct than to invent. To get my imagination going I would rather look at an old photograph, a discolored popular painting, or a bundle of yellowish letters than to depend on my soap bubble dreams. Therefore, I had an urge to see, smell, hear, and take in with all my senses the land itself where the glorious deed had taken place. And so, conquering my drowsiness typical of an old middle class doctor, at an age past seventy I undertook the trip leading to the historical site" (III, 1102). Seeing with his own eyes the Fuerte del Sombrero was the only way Azuela could reconstruct the historical events about which he writes in this work.

Rarely did Azuela place the action of his novels in an environment that was not his native state of Jalisco or Mexico City. Part of *La mujer domada* takes place in Morelia, capital of the state of Michoacán, south of Jalisco, and on the road between Guadalajara and Mexico City. Another exception is found in *Avanzada* where he moves his characters, in the second part, from Jalisco to the state of Veracruz, where the action takes place in the sugar-cane fields and mills. Again, the second part of *Sendas perdidas* takes place in the state of Oaxaca, and in *Nueva burguesía* there is a brief description of the landscape in the state of Querétaro.

Not all of the scenes in Azuela's novels take place in the open fields or in the streets of Mexico City. He liked to place scenes in reduced quarters, such as a railroad car, as in *Las moscas, El camarada Pantoja* and *El desquite;* in hospitals, as in *La Malhora;* and in government offices, as in *Regina Landa* and *La maldición.* Equally important are his descriptions of local celebrations and amusements, such as bullfights, cockfights, horse races, rodeos, popular fiestas, religious ceremonies, and local and national customs such as popular dances and holidays. These descriptions give his novels a colorful note and make them truly national. With the many changes Mexico has undergone during the last few years, these sketches will undoubtedly help the reader to visualize a world which is fast becoming a thing of the past.

It is typical of Azuela's technique to intermingle with the human environment descriptions of nature. These passages are always short, well integrated into the narrative, and in consonance with the nature of the characters. The fusion of man and landscape is characteristic of his style, as there is always an intimate relation between man and nature, and in nature between the landscape and animal life. As a rule, nature is humanized, which makes human actions appear either insignificant or ennobled. Gertrudis' song in *Mala yerba,* for instance, is given a magic air by comparing it to that of the dove singing in the willow grove and that of the moaning wind that fans the elm's rigid branches, "a voice lost among the thousand voices with which the fields express their infinite sadness" (I, 179).

This humanizing of the lower forms of life makes ferocious human acts appear much more inhuman. When Azuela describes a cockfight he tells the reader that the struggle has "an almost human ferocity" (I, 411). The contrast between a humanized

animal and a dehumanized man is well presented in this scene from
Las moscas:

> Dawn approaches; a ray of light, gleaming like diamonds, appears
> in the East. Gusts of cold wind pass through the open doors. Some
> men turn over half asleep and grunt insolences. Mr. Ríos wakes up
> and snorts dryly, like a horse with a cold. . . . On a straw heap a
> rooster with a comb as red as a blood clot and fiery golden feathers
> proudly lifts its stately head, shakes its wings, raises its beak, and like
> a bugler in the field emits a harsh, shrill song that rends the air. (II,
> 882)

Compared to the grandiose nature of the landscape, man in
Azuela's novels always appears to be small and insignificant,
almost as a protruding part of that same nature. In *Mala yerba*
there is first a description of the landscape: "Down below rise
the large rocks like gigantic slices of crystalized silex; farther
below, the valley spreads out" (I, 206). Then man appears, like
an insignificant ant when contrasted to the greatness of the landscape: "And in that vast field . . . a yoke of oxen carry behind
them a small figure leaning over the handle of the plough and
leaving behind him the black furrow" (*ibid.*).

In some novels, like *Los de abajo,* the fusion of man and nature
reaches a high degree of perfection. The scene at the end of this
novel, in which Azuela describes the death of Macías, is perhaps
the best example. At the end of *Las moscas* Villa's defeat is also
described in terms of the fusion of man and nature. In spite of
his excellent descriptions of nature, Azuela felt that the writer is
never able to re-create its greatness: "The truth is that the soul
of man expands in front of a landscape in the same measure that
it contracts in front of a book" (II, 328).

II *The Characters*

After creating the stage, Azuela continues: "Suddenly I am the
witness to a marvelous phenomenon . . . from that shapeless mass
of words and phrases gradually the characters, like figures in a
Chinese box, begin to appear" (III, 1043). This power to create
characters had already been attested to by the perceptive Mexican
critic, Xavier Villaurrutia: "In Azuela we do not admire so
much his economy and the simplicity of his means, as the speed
with which he can create. A few phrases and we are already in

the midst of an atmosphere; a few lines, which last only a second, and a character is already on its feet; and in the same manner another and another." [1]   By what process was he able to breathe life into his characters?

Azuela learned the technique of characterization in the novels of the French realists and naturalists of the nineteenth century: Balzac, Zola, and Maupassant. Following Zola's dictum, he copied directly from life, keeping a notebook in which he annotated the features of interesting men and women he met. Often he combined the characteristics of two or three of these persons. In his student years he liked "to follow the first extravagant fellow he met on the street, in the arcade, in church, or no matter where . . . he would not leave him until he had obtained all the information he needed about his life . . . after a few years the vagabond student had catalogued every living being in Guadalajara who had a queer personality. In the serenades he would take a seat near the common people in order to hear, with delight, their conversations." [2] Years later he was to do the same thing with the soldiers and officers he accompanied during the revolutionary period; and in Mexico City, with the patients that visited the clinic where he worked and the office he had installed at home.

In his first novel, *María Luisa,* he portrayed his fellow medical students and also a patient in the hospital. A high school student served as a model for one of the male characters, Pancho, and Chato reflects the personality of a medical student, or rather a pseudo-student skillful in deceiving the freshmen at cards. In the technique of contrasting the good and the bad in his characters, he followed the examples of Dumas and Prévost, especially the latter's *Manon Lescaut.*

In the novels of this early period most of the characters are portraits of persons actually living in the city of Lagos. The protagonist of *Los fracasados* reflects the personality of the parish priest, whom Azuela had met in the Seminario Conciliar of Guadalajara; the Secretary in the City Hall, Attorney Reséndez, is a faithful picture of Azuela's friend, the poet José Becerra. Most of the characters in *Mala yerba,* the novelist confessed, were drawn from people he had met while practicing medicine in his native town and surrounding area. To introduce an exotic note, he makes use of a character of foreign extraction (the only one in his novels), the North American Mr. John, an engineer who takes Marcela away from Julián.

The same José Becerra who inspired Azuela to create the character of Reséndez in *Los fracasados* reappears in his first novel of the revolution, *Andrés Pérez, maderista,* as the hero of the novel, the revolutionary Toño Reyes. He reappears in *Los caciques* as Rodríguez and in *Los de abajo* as Valderrama. These characters, being copies of the same living person, do not differ much in personality, except in the case of Valderrama, who is much more eccentric than the others. In Andrés Pérez, Azuela introduced a character that was to reappear frequently in his works; the antihero, Andrés Pérez, representing the intellectual from Mexico City, is a precursor of Luis Cervantes in *The Underdogs.*

In the novels published before *Los de abajo,* characterization is weak due to Azuela's insistence on creating characters in opposition representing good and evil; the good characters are flawless and the evil ones are all evil. As a revolutionary and in contact with people from all social classes and from all regions, Azuela made a great discovery. He wrote: "Men who are all good or all bad exist only in novels" (III, 1060). From here on he forgot the French models and created characters that are a true reflection of men, neither thoroughly good nor thoroughly evil. The protagonist of *Los de abajo,* Demetrio Macías, represents a new trend in characterization. He is human to the point of being excessively kind to the enemy at times and cruel to his own men at other times. He does not represent, like the heroes in previous novels, a single living person. To draw him, Azuela combined the personalities of two revolutionary leaders, General Julián Medina and Colonel Manuel Caloca. This was not, however, planned from the start. First, Azuela drew upon the person of Medina, but when he met the young officer, Manuel Caloca, in Guadalajara, he forgot about Medina. "I paid no further attention to Medina in order to shape and mold with entire liberty the character I had imagined. Manuel Caloca, the youngest member of a revolutionary family from Teúl, state of Zacatecas, about twenty years of age, tall, slender, with features slightly mongoloid, gay and fearless, brave in battle to the point of recklessness, succeeded Julián Medina in the creation of my character" (III, 1080).

Luis Cervantes, second in importance to Macías, has often been thought to represent the novelist himself. Nothing could be further from the truth; Luis Cervantes had been a medical student and became a medic in Macías' army, but here the similarity ends. Of Cervantes, Azuela had this to say: "Luis Cervantes is an imaginary person, built upon other imaginary persons and a few traits taken from reality" (III, 1082). These traits taken from reality reflect some of the characteristics of Francisco M. Delgado, private secretary of Medina and a person not too well liked by Azuela. "It was not, of course, the real Delgado, but the image of Delgado as created by slander, that character that I needed for my novel, the character named Luis Cervantes" (III, 1083).

To portray minor characters in *Los de abajo,* which are so important, Azuela drew directly upon the men he had met while serving as an army surgeon with Medina. Antonio Montañés represents Medina's friend and companion, Pedro Montes, an officer on the staff at headquarters. El Güero Margarito represents a waiter Azuela met in Ciudad Juárez at the Delmonico Restaurant, an extremely unpleasant fellow. Azuela described him in this manner: short, with a round red face, fat-cheeked and blood-shot eyes. "He was very active, boasted of knowing personally the most famous revolutionary leaders and, at the same time, treated us civilians with scorn and even insolence. Out of this hateful person, El Güero Margarito was born, a character I rounded out with features from other persons, such as Colonel Galván, an habitual drunk . . . [and] another Colonel who joined Medina's forces after the *carrancistas* took Guadalajara. He was a big man, almost apoplectic, of red hair and beard, extremely irritable. When he became angry, he would pull out hairs from his beard until he bled. Near the town of Tequila, he was wounded in one knee by a bullet. When he tried to get up and couldn't, he drew his revolver and shot himself in the head" (III, 1083).

No less extravagant are the personalities of those utilized by Azuela to portray other characters appearing in his famous novel. Venancio represents a quack doctor who joined Medina's forces in the town of Hostotipaquillo. La Pintada was a girl companion of Colonel Maximiano Hernández, a dark-complexioned woman who used heavy makeup on her lips, eyes, and cheeks. Pancracio, whose real name was Barbarito, was a soldier in Medina's army. Some of his companions, La Codorniz, El Manteca, and El Meco, were also common soldiers whose names were not even changed when they passed from real life to the novel. They were, Azuela says of them, "anonymous soldiers, cannon fodder, poor people who did not even use the name with which they were baptized. They went through life like those dry leaves swept by the wind" (III, 1085). In spite of this, each one of them, in the novel, has his own personality and acts according to his will.

Azuela had little to say about the women appearing in the novel, except for La Pintada. It is known that Camila was the name of a servant in Azuela's home in Lagos de Moreno and that a character bearing the same name appears in the short story "En derrota." But Azuela does not say that this girl was the prototype for the character in *Los de abajo*. He only said: "Camila and the other women were of my own invention and were created as they were needed in the structure of the book" (III, 1086).

As is to be expected, some of the characters of *The Underdogs* reappear in later novels. Pascual, in *Las tribulaciones . . .* is very much like Luis Cervantes; Captain Covarrubias, in the same novel, reminds the reader of the young officer who was in charge of defending the town taken by Macías and his men. Indeed, one of the few original characters appearing in *Las tribulaciones . . .* is Procopio, a character who goes through an experience not unlike that endured by the author himself.

Characterization in Azuela's novels is based on the use of the portrait, giving emphasis to the physical characteristics, supplemented by realistic dialogue and significant actions. In *La Luciérnaga,* however, the technique differs somewhat. Here the author makes an effort to analyze the psychology of the characters. The reader is placed in the minds of Dionisio and José María and is able to follow their thinking and become acquainted with the motives that make them act the way they do. Unfortunately, Azuela does not follow the same technique in the novels written after *La Luciérnaga,* in which he returns to the well-tried method used previously. He firmly believed that by avoiding the psychological portrait and creating flat, plain characters he could reach a larger reading public, who, he thought, would not be interested in new techniques. But even so, he was a master at creating characters by providing only a few outstanding features.

Azuela was able to breathe life into his creations by immediately giving the reader the outstanding individual features by means of which the character could be recognized and remembered. This technique has its drawbacks, as often the portrait turns out to be a caricature, especially in cases where the novelist paints persons he detested. To them he often gave animal features, perhaps due to the influences of the Naturalistic novelists. Even a character like Camila, who is portrayed with sympathy, is compared to "a monkey wearing a skirt." Another of his characters has a chimpanzee face, and Father Jeremías (in *Los caciques*) has a head like that of an armadillo. In *Las moscas* there is a man with a bulldog face, and the Minister of Public Instruction looks like an angora cat. The caricature stage is reached in this novel when the author characterizes a man named Rubén as a gorilla with glasses, and General Malacara as a man with the brain of a bird. But it is in the characterization of General Xicoténcatl Robespierre (in *Domitilo quiere ser diputado*) where Azuela pours out all his dislike for military officers. He is presented as being vain, stupid, and ignorant. Although women are usually portrayed with a sympathetic eye, in *Las tribulaciones . . .* we find perhaps Azuela's most repugnant creation. Doña Aurora Caloca de Tabardillo, a go-between, is compared to a filthy and blotched red owl.

Often, by attributing to his characters the features of more than one animal, Azuela creates real monsters. El Chicharrón in *Avanzada* has the snout of a pig and the eyes of a fish. This combination of pig and fish is common in Azuela. In *La mujer domada* there is a policeman, "a kind of pig because of his hairy face, and a batrachian because of the shape of his mouth" (II, 306). But the best example of a monster is perhaps a character named Alcayata (Spike) in the novel *Avanzada;* he has the features of a monkey, a cat, and a dog. "His body was slippery and shiny like that of a monkey, he was a fawning female cat with his superiors, his small eyes resembled those of a chihuahua dog, and his voice was similar to the noise produced by a drill; hearing him talk actually caused physical pain" (I, 1055).

Often, when Azuela wanted to present a person in a ridiculous light, instead of comparing him to an animal, he attributed to him some characteristic pertaining to the plant kingdom. Thus there are persons whose heads resemble a tomato, an ear of corn, a chickpea, an onion; persons whose cheeks are like the dried rind of a sour orange; with a set of teeth like corn on the cob; with a nose like a mango; a face like a quince or a dried fig.[3]

No less important than the characterizations based on anthropological characteristics are those based on medical analyses. Azuela, the doctor, could not help conceiving his characters as sick people or at least as suffering from some illness. Rare is the novel in which the reader does not find at least one doctor or a student of medicine. Often the character is seen with a clinical eye and remains as a representative of some illness or physical defect. In *María Luisa* there is Chato, whose eyelids have been eaten away by scrofula. Toño, in *Los fracasados,* suffers from *jiricua* (discoloration of the skin). Domitilo, the man who wants to be a representative in Congress, is a cretin. In *El camarada Pantoja* there is a colonel who is an alcoholic and whose nostrils have been eaten away by syphilis. And in one of his last novels, *La maldición,* one of the characters is so squint-eyed that he cannot look anyone straight in the face.

In characterizing, Azuela paid special attention to the tone of voice of his characters. He went out of his way to look for adjectives and adjectival phrases to describe a voice. The voice of a person may be distinguished by its singsong manner, by the quality of its tone, or by its strident nature. A voice may have a nasal twang, or may be clear, emphatic, high pitched and penetrating, or sound like the bark of a chihuahua dog or the cackle of a chicken with pip.[4] As important as the physical portrait is the characterization accomplished, always with great effect, through dialogue. Azuela knew well the characteristic speech of each social class and used speech effectively in each character according to his social class, his region, and his profession. An exception is found in *Esa sangre,* where Julián sometimes speaks like an Argentinean gaucho, a dialect with which Azuela was not familiar. Important also is the characterization based on the actions of the men and women appearing in the novels, the use of names and especially nicknames, the frequent association of tics and mannerisms to a character, and the use of certain features taken from well-known figures in the world of the arts or in the real world. The following examples will give an idea of the primary sources of secondary images used by Azuela to characterize: "At that moment a man appeared dressed in black, he looked pale, and his beard was long and black also: let us say, a silhouette pulled out from one of Greco's canvasses" (I, 710); Don Cuco, a newspaperman, looks like "an insolent dwarf, taken from one of Velázquez'

pictures" (II, 780); María, in the novel *Andrés Pérez, maderista,*
"has a tragic head, as if it had been pulled out of an illustration by
Juan Lorraine" (II, 777); Chata, in *El camarada Pantoja,* has
"slanting eyes, very much like those painted by Diego Rivera"
(I, 683); De Anda, in *La maldición,* has "a face like that of San
Luis Gonzaga" (II, 538). For the Mexican reader, this last image
is quite effective, as he is well acquainted with the face of this
famous saint.

All this may give the impression that Azuela's characterizations
are always done in negative terms, but this is not so. There are
persons in his novels drawn with sympathy. Normal characters
are as common as the abnormal or queer. It seems, however, that
his genius for characterizing shines when the drawing is negative.
In both cases he had the ability to select the details necessary to
give the reader, in a few lines, a precise idea of the character. The
French critic, Valéry Larbaud, had this to say about Azuela as a
creator of fictitious characters: "He never judges the acts of his
characters, he never tells us what he thinks about them, nor what
he wants the reader to think, either about the person or his acts.
All his efforts are directed toward letting us see them as they
appear in front of him, and in this eagerness to capture the truth
in life lies his moral nature as an artist, the supreme virtue not
only of the painter but also of the novelist, since it can be applied
to both the interior man as well as the exterior man or to the
landscape." [5]

III *Plots*

Once he had set the stage and created the characters, Azuela
turned to the plot. As he wrote in his autobiography, the plot
in his novels is always subordinated to the characters:

> Just like a baby who begins to walk, I take the characters by the
> hand and help them along, but only as far as to place them securely
> in the direction that they themselves want to take. I do not force
> them. I only help them avoid the first stumbling blocks they may find
> in their way, and prevent them from leaving the tracks. Soon they
> do not need me and from that moment on my mission is pleasantly
> reduced to that of a simple stenographer: they speak and I write what
> they say. I let them do whatever they want and only try to have them
> express themselves with clarity. (III, 1043)

The above quotation is revealing, for it explains why, in Azuela's novels, background and characters stand out, while plot and structure are weak. His works are usually structured around characters. The novel can begin without the author having a definite plan in mind. The interesting point for him is character development, often at the cost of neglecting the unfolding of the plot. Even the titles of his novels reflect this interest in his characters: his first novel, *María Luisa,* has the title of the heroine; the same thing happens with *Regina Landa, La Malhora, La Marchanta,* and even *La Luciérnaga,* although here the reference is not too clear. In other novels the name of the protagonist also appears in the title: *Andrés Pérez, maderista; El camarada Pantoja, Domitilo quiere ser diputado.* And in some novels the title refers to the protagonist or protagonists, although the name is not given: *Los fracasados, La mujer domada, Esa sangre.* The exception is found when the title refers to the social group and not the protagonist or any specific character: *Mala yerba, Los de abajo, Los caciques, Las moscas, Nueva burguesía.* Azuela's purpose in the use of titles is to fix the reader's attention upon the characters, around which the plot unfolds.

The characters are taken, as has been demonstrated, from the writer's contemporary world. This of necessity dictates the time of the action and even the theme and nature of the subject matter. Azuela was primarily interested, as he himself wrote, "in what is throbbing and moving around us—life. Life without deformations or stylizations; life, complete and totally" (III, 1056). That is why he wrote about a medical case when he was a medical student; about life in a small town when he returned to Lagos to practice his profession; about rural life when he became acquainted with its structure as a rural doctor; about the revolution when he was an army doctor with Villa's lieutenants; about life in the poorer sections of Mexico City when he became acquainted with it as a doctor in one of the city's worst slums; about the life of the bureaucrats when he held a position in one of the secretariats. Except for the short trip into the past history of Mexico, he always wrote about what was in front of him, be it in the country, in the small town, or in the capital. This is the element that gives his novels the value of a social document, a report by the hand of an honest and conscientious personal witness.

From the throbbing life around him Azuela usually selected

those elements that had dramatic possibilities. These he found in the struggle between the social classes or social groups. In *Mala yerba* it is between the peons and the domineering, almost feudal, landlords. It must be emphasized, however, that this struggle is presented in social and not racial terms. The racial conflict, although latent, is never spotlighted by Azuela. He never divided Mexican society into Indians, mestizos, and whites, but rather into those that exploit and are exploited, into the underdogs and the "upperdogs," into victims and sacrificial priests. The picture he presents of the Mexican society is never that of an anthropologist or sociologist but rather that of a physician who sees only the endemic illnesses affecting that society, which need to be eradicated in order to bring the society back to a healthy state.

Azuela's early novels reflect an interest in personal illness and in personal maladjustments. Beginning with *Los caciques* there is a change from this interest in individual cases to an interest in group behavior, and finally to social change and national problems: the revolution, the downfall of the feudal regime, the creation of a new social class.

In the novels of his last period Azuela's interest changes again. Instead of being an objective recorder of social change, he becomes a stern critic of the new social order and is thus less effective as a novelist.

IV *Structure*

Of all the elements that go into the making of a novel, Azuela paid least attention to its structure. This is perhaps the weakest point in his narrative technique. He very seldom had a plan of the whole novel before he sat down to write it. In the following pages an attempt will be made to analyze the structure of Azuela's novels. In order to trace its development, the novels will be discussed in chronological order.

In the structure of Azuela's first novel, *María Luisa,* no well thought-out plan can be detected. Since the novel is an enlarged short story, its structure suffers from lack of balance: the hasty denouement clashes with the slow unfolding of the action. Once María Luisa has been seduced the action stops abruptly, and there is a violent change. The transition between the scenes depicting her fall and her death (which happens three years later) is not well developed. These three important years in María

Luisa's life, during which she becomes a human wreck, are brushed aside with a few statements by the author. Rather than a novel, this first work is a long, drawn-out short story.

Los fracasados, unlike *María Luisa,* has the structure of a true novel. It is divided into eighteen short numbered chapters without titles. But there are still some structural defects. At the end of Chapter 5, the Secretary of the city government begins to tell the story of Consuelo. The story is continued in the following chapter, but the reader is unaware, until the end, that it is the author and not the secretary who is talking. This inconsistency appears in the following novel, *Mala yerba,* in which a great improvement in narrative technique is noticeable. Here for the first time Azuela uses effectively the point of view of one of the characters. The history of the Andrade family is not told by the omniscient author but by one of the persons in the novel, Señor Pablo, thus giving it a more realistic perspective and making it much more acceptable to the reader. Although there are some digressions, for instance, the painting of some local customs, the action unfolds evenly and terminates logically in a tragic end. The scenes are very well integrated and the transition from one to another well designed. The descriptions of nature, for the first time, are well adapted to plot development and do not detract from the unfolding of the action. There is unity of place, and the passing of time is well worked-out. Unity of action is accomplished by focusing the reader's attention upon the central figures, Marcela and Julián.

The above cannot be said about *Sin amor,* where there seems to be a regression in technique. The slow unfolding of the plot lacks a forceful ending. Azuela made use of the worn out structure of the realistic Spanish novels he was so fond of reading, without making any effort to be original. Fortunately for his next novel, *Andrés Pérez, maderista,* he abandoned this stale structure and attempted something new. For the first time he used the first-person narrative throughout the novel, letting the protagonist tell his own story. The weak structural point of this work is found in the denouement since the novel does not end with the tragic death of Toño, but with Andrés' betrayal of his best friend. Here Azuela sacrificed a dramatic climax to better portray a scoundrel. His interest in characterization leads him to weaken the structure of his novel.

No great progress in technique is noticed in *Los caciques*. Its ending, however, is much more dramatic than that of *Andrés Pérez*. . . . This dramatic element makes the critics think that at the time of writing the novel the author already had in mind the idea of writing the play. Its division into three parts was easily adapted to the theater. Even the subtitle, *Del Llano Hermanos, S. en C.* (title used in the play adaptation), suggests Azuela's intention. With this work, Azuela's period as apprentice in the art of the novel comes to an end. He is now ready to write his best work, in which he is to put into practice all he has learned. The novel ends when the revolution begins, in a scene which is symbolic of a new era in the author's life and also in the political and social life of Mexico.

From the point of view of its structure, *Los de abajo* can be considered as Azuela's best planned novel. Divided into three symmetrical parts (21, 14, and 7 chapters), the novel opens with a scene in the Cañón de Juchipila. From here until the end of the second part the action increases progressively, both in violence and in dramatic intensity. For the rebels there is nothing but easy victories and rich spoils. The third part opens with a letter written by Luis Cervantes from El Paso which serves, because of its humorous tone, as an interlude in the grim drama of the revolution. Up to this point Macías has been fortunate, but in the third part his good luck changes and nothing turns out right for him. The novel ends with his death in the same Cañón de Juchipila where he had so soundly beaten the enemy in the opening scenes. The wheel of fortune has completed its full circle. "Los de abajo" return to their position, both physically and socially, from which they had started. This closed structure is similar to a *bola,* a ball, which makes the reader think of a revolution, called *la bola* in Mexico.

The novel's structure does not have the precise planning found in other great Latin American novels. It is not, like Romulo Gallegos' *Doña Bárbara,* a novel with a logical structure, with its thesis, antithesis, and synthesis. Rather than logical, the structure of *The Underdogs* is organic. Although it may be a chaotic story (a well-ordered picture of a revolution is unthinkable), the structure is very well suited to the theme, and thus Azuela is able to lift the work to an esthetic plane where, under an apparent disorder, the reader finds an internal, organic order in which there are no loose scenes, no actions without a proper function in the apparently dissonant whole. As an organism, the novel is characterized by its dynamic essence, which is to be found not only in the plot, but also in the style, in the painting of nature, and in the violent quality of the scenes, not too far distant from those painted by José Clemente Orozco.

The structure of *Los de abajo* is an innovation in Spanish American narrative. Azuela, either consciously or unconsciously, created a new form for the Latin American novel, a form that for the first time reflects the nature of the world where it was born. For the first time the novelist forgets the European forms and writes a novel in which the theme and structure complement each other. Azuela's work begins a new trend in the development of the Spanish American novel. For the critics who have thought that *Los de abajo* is a product of an artist unconscious of his craft, the following statement by the author may come as a surprise: "The novelist surely takes the elements that go into his work from the world around him or from books. But such a work is not limited to the simple accumulation and organization of the inert materials of which it is built; they must be structured into a creative work, into a new body having its own life" (III, 1082).

The first edition of *The Underdogs* bears the subtitle *Sketches and Scenes of the Present Revolution.* This subtitle is also used in the novels *Las moscas* and *Domitilo quiere ser diputado,* published in one volume with the short story "De como al fin lloró Juan Pablo." *Las moscas,* unlike *Los de abajo,* is indeed a collection of loosely integrated sketches and scenes. It has in common with *The Underdogs,* however, a dynamic element not to be found in a simple collection of sketches. Except for the last, which is a true plastic painting of Villa in defeat, all the scenes are characterized by their movement: the restlessness of the crowd at the station; the trip in the military train; General Malacara's pleasure drive through the streets of Irapuato. In the background, there is the restless movement of the revolutionary troops, already defeated and only thinking of escaping with their lives. Although there is hardly any unifying narrative thread, the unity in this novel is achieved through the presence of the same characters, symbolic of the many factions and opinions that go into the forming of a revolutionary army like that of Francisco Villa.

The style of the novels of the revolution closes with *Las tribulaciones* . . . , a work structured in two parts, "The Book of Bitter Hours" and "Procopio's Triumph." The break in structure between these two parts is complete. The first part, very much like *Andrés Pérez,* is told by one of the characters in the novel, in this case César, Procopio's younger son. In the second part César has disappeared (he has died, although the reader does not know it until later), and the omniscient author continues with the narrative. There is also a noticeable change of tone between the parts, the first being much more serene and peaceful than the second. Perhaps Azuela changed the point of view to better express his indignation toward the unnecessary quarreling among the revolutionary leaders, and especially toward those persons who without actually having fought were now in possession of the movement. It is true that the second part is much more emotive, and the novelist's rage cannot be mistaken. But what is gained in emotive power is lost in unity by the abrupt change in point of view. The reader receives the impression of reading two novels, although the characters (with few exceptions) are the same. By speaking through César in the first part, Azuela was able to see things objectively. In the second part he becomes much more subjective, although speaking in the third person. Unfortunately, this structural defect prevents this otherwise good novel from reaching the heights of *Los de abajo*.

Perhaps the fact that Azuela had been ignored by the critics made him abandon the technique he had used in his novels of the revolution and try something new. The novels written during this period are interesting experiments in the use of new structures. In the first of these novels, *La Malhora,* Azuela for the first time makes use of the dislocated structure, characterized by the over-lapping of the time element, the fragmentary scene, the flashback, the disrupted plot, and unfinished characterization. The most striking change in technique is the use of juxtaposed scenes, un-related by logical links. The spatial arrangement makes this novel one of the most difficult to read. It opens with the murder of La Malhora's father, an action which is not made clear until the last chapter. It is at the end, too, that the reader first becomes aware that the killer is also the man who had abused La Malhora and led her into a life of prostitution.

Although this short novel is divided into four parts, each with a different background, it does not lose its unity, which is preserved by a return at the end to the locale of the first scenes. Perhaps a reader unacquainted with the structure of the picaresque novel may find the unfolding of the plot somewhat chaotic. It is obvious that Azuela had in mind the picaresque structure, as he has La Malhora pass from master to master in a series of otherwise unrelated scenes. The presence of the protagonist, as is customary in the picaresque novel, unifies the work and gives the author, at the same time, the opportunity to focus upon several social groups in different parts of the city. As in *Los de abajo,* the action begins and ends in the same place. Unlike *Los de abajo,* the structure is not circular, but rather quadrangular. The four episodes in the life of the young prostitute, trivial in themselves, reflect a consciousness on the part of the author to make use of geometrical structure, a novelty in Mexican fiction. It is for this reason that *La Malhora* points the way to a new type of novel.

With *El desquite,* the second experimental novel, Azuela was less successful. The story, narrated by a doctor in Mexico City, loses its dramatic impact when the action passes from the capital to the provinces. Compared with *La Malhora,* its structure is rather weak due to the unnecessary scenes, such as the one in the bullring which has no function except to describe a favorite Mexican sport. Much more damaging than the unrelated scenes is the weak outcome, which leaves the reader in a state of bewilderment. The novel lacks the structural balance found in *Los de abajo* or *La Malhora.*

It is not until Azuela writes *La Luciérnaga* that he is able to retain unity while at the same time employing the technique of using two locales, Mexico City and a town in the provinces. Two of the principal characters, Dionisio and his brother José María, are separated in space. However, Azuela passes from the mind of the first to that of the second without formal and unnecessary explanations. His transfer seems natural, and the reader is even unaware of the change. Dionisio, drunk in Mexico City, sinks like an' Atlas under the pillow of his bed.

Life and time go back months, years . . . Who? A monk inquisitor?

The hell's porter? . . . All right, all right, brother José María, let's not exaggerate! . . .
José María, a just and pious gentleman, a good citizen of Cieneguilla. His face, ascetic, his gestures, very serious, his lines, inexorable. Well, José María speaks, and speaks . . .
"Yes, brother Dionisio, I am José María himself [. . .]" (I, 569).

In addition to this psychological device, Azuela makes use of another technique, the vision. By means of the vision he is able to shift scenes without having to move the characters physically from one place to another and without losing continuity. Dionisio was in Mexico City and at the same time, by means of cryptaestesia, or perhaps due to a simple nightmare, José María, in his bed, in his home in Cieneguilla, three hundred kilometers from Mexico City, had a vision of his brother, Dionisio, and his family and how they were struggling in poverty, owing to his miserliness.

The novel, divided into five parts, presents a bipolar structure. Just as there are two stages where the action takes place (Mexico City and Cieneguilla), there are two protagonists (Dionisio and José María) placed in opposition to each other: Dionisio is swallowed up by the big city, and José María is devoured by his own greed. To integrate these two themes Azuela introduces María Cristina, Dionisio's daughter, who, although living in Mexico City with her family, is not destroyed by the city but by the avarice of her uncle, José María. *La Luciérnaga* was one of Azuela's most successful novels. Much of this success, it is believed, was due to the care he gave to the structure of the work. In spite of this he abandoned the new technique, and his subsequent novels were written in traditional forms. None of his novels after *La Luciérnaga,* except perhaps *Nueva burguesía,* presents any technical innovations or any new experiments with form or structure.[6]

V *Style*

In the development of Azuela's style there are four well-defined periods: first there is the style of the early novels, from *María Luisa* to *Sin amor;* then the style typical of the novels of the revolution; this is followed by the period of the experimental novels, in which Azuela consciously writes in a different style; and, last, the period during which he reverted to the use of former stylistic devices.

In the writing of his first novels Azuela tried to imitate the style of the French and Spanish Naturalists. Gradually he began to create his own style, characterized by simplicity in sentence structure, brief descriptions of the landscape, and increased use of dialogue. His style is the result of his concept of the novel. For him it was not necessary to be a great stylist in order to be a good novelist, and he believed that the novelist who is overly conscious of style loses other essential qualities necessary in the good novel. For this reason he would never sacrifice a clear description of reality for the sake of style. Speaking of *El santo horror,* a novel by Martín Gómez Palacio, Azuela had this to say: "What most surprises me about his novel is that, being the work of a poet, it is exempt of *literature.* (I write *literature* in italics to give it the special meaning that it has in France, where it is used to denote a style that is made up of empty words, sonorous phrases and sentences, which are as sonorous as they are empty)" (III, 683–84). Azuela refused to write in this bombastic style and preferred simple, straightforward, clear expression.

This simplicity does not imply that Azuela's style is childish or primitive. On the contrary, it reveals a great effort on his part to write clearly and without stylish mannerisms. On this point he wrote: "It is a much more difficult task to write with clarity and simplicity, keeping the attention of the reader, than getting on the bandwagon and trying to attract attention by imitating the capers of a medicine man" (III, 1121). Azuela was firmly convinced that stylistic simplicity is essential to a good novel.

Azuela obtains simplicity by avoiding the use of learned, unfamiliar words. Nevertheless, he never lacks the proper words to convey his thoughts to the reader or to describe things vividly. As the poet Xavier Villarrutia expressed it: "He never looked around for words, but he always found them." [7] This observation indicates that the novelist used in his writings the popular speech he had learned directly from experience, whether at home, on the farm, or in the city slums. Since his main preoccupation was to capture in his novels the flavor of the Mexican scene, this popular speech was sufficient, and he could afford the luxury of avoiding literary language. Thus, one of the striking stylistic features in Azuela is the large number of words, idioms, and expressions taken from the popular speech of the people, that is, from Mexican

Spanish. He believed that through speech, people reveal their souls and innermost ways of being.

Azuela's sentence structure is characterized by its straight-forward nature, obtained by eliminating or reducing the use of subordinate clauses. The majority of his sentences are short, without complicated syntactical elaborations. His rule seems to be to follow the shortest path in the building of the sentence. This syntactical brevity, which imparts a great force to his style, was what made the French critic Larbaud think of Tacitus when reading Azuela.

In *Los de abajo,* the novel in which Azuela reached his highest stylistic accomplishment, the reader can best observe the several techniques which the novelist used to give his style a seal of its own. There he will find the use of very short paragraphs, the predominance of dialogue over description, the use of expressions typical of the Spanish of Mexico, the brief, almost schematic, descriptions of the landscape, and the use of a rhythmical pattern that reflects the violent nature of the subject matter. This style, which is to be found in other novels of Azuela, especially in those written during this period in his development as a novelist, is the most original and the one the reader associates with his name. It seems that he himself recognized this fact, as he wrote: "The authors that most influenced me during my literary beginnings, almost to the exclusion of any others, were Balzac, Zola, Flaubert, the Goncourt Brothers, and Daudet. After my first four novels I continued to write under the influence of the contemporary French novelists, until my books were related to the Revolution. When I wrote these I do not believe I was touched by any other influences" (III, 1280).

Since his novels of the revolution, and indeed all his novels, had been ignored by the critics, Azuela decided to experiment with a new style. There is no question about this being the motivating force behind the decision to change his way of writing. In his autobiography he makes this point explicitly clear; he wrote: "Tired of being an author known only in my own home, I made the brave resolution to attract the attention of the public by writing according to the latest technique. I studied that technique carefully and came to the conclusion that it consists simply in the use of the now well-known trick of distorting words and phrases, of deliberately making concepts and expressions obscure to obtain the effect of novelty" (III, 1113). Although Azuela is talking about technique, he has in mind stylistic innovations and not those of narrative structure. As an example of a tortuous style he quotes a paragraph from a Central American novel, and then he expresses the same thing in two lines (O.C. III, 1113–14).

Although in his new novels he abandons his customary way of writing, he continues to use popular speech as much as possible. "In spite of the novelty of the procedure," he wrote, "I tried to keep with tenacity something which, good or bad, I have invariably included in my novels, that is, the popular language, intentionally used even in that part narrated by myself, a habit which traditional critics have often held against me, a criticism I have learned to ignore" (III, 1115).

Soon after the writing of *La Malhora*, which was rejected by the judges of a novel contest, Azuela became famous with the "discovery" of *Los de abajo* by Professor Francisco Monterde. Encouraged by this unexpected taste of fame, he wrote *El desquite* and then *La Luciérnaga*, the latter being his greatest literary triumph. After these novels, however, he abandoned his new style. Why? He explains it this way in his autobiography: "After the incomplete success of *La Luciérnaga*, a work in which I escaped from myself (as has been aptly said by a second-rate critic who thinks that genius is manifested by writing in a distorted way), I made a thorough examination of my conscience and found myself guilty. I felt ashamed of having used the now worn-out trick of twisting phrases to give the impression of being intelligent, ingenious, and clever. I recognize the fact that when a writer expresses himself clearly, he is apt to be called a fool. But to me that is much more honest, much more decent" (III, 1118).

The style Azuela used in his new novels does not show as radical a departure from the old style as he himself thought. Certainly there is a greater novelty in the structure of these novels than in the style, which seems to be a logical development of the one used in *Los de abajo*, and especially in the short story, "El caso López Romero," written in 1916. The stylistic innovations consist of the use of distorted sentences, the omission of the main verb in the sentence, and the use of indirect discourse. In *La Malhora* there are several impressionistic descriptions, like the following:

[The saloon] El Vacilón was full to the brim. The jolly laughter of the mandolins, the grumble of Don Apolonio's guitar, the *Pure*

Flowers of El Flaco, the very popular tenor from Tepito. O wave of soiled rags, insolvent as royal cloaks; pear-shaped heads like *chayotes,* pitch-black; sinister merry faces; shining of feline pupils, and the shivering whiteness of paper, a harsh contrast of lines and shades, and endless disintegration of masses and reliefs. (II, 953)

There is also the characteristic use of words in a series, juxtaposed without the customary syntactical connecting links, as can be observed in the following quotations:

Handcuffs, gags, steel springs on the inverted neck. Iron, cold, flesh, bone, all in one. (II, 962)
The Gutierrez from Irapuato—an emphysematic mother, two daughters approaching their forties, cockroach-colored cone-shaped shawls, blue ribbon, wide and reptant skirts, low heels—one day hear it said that. . . . (II, 967)

The same procedure is used to describe Tepito's market, Mexico City's poorest:

A concert of harsh notes, rotten roofs and heaps and heaps of trash next to quarter pounds of vegetables and crumbling hills of cereals. "Nickels, they are nickels of pumice stone." Dishevelled heads, the croaking of parked wagons, the blow of the ax that rends the gamy meat apart, the ragged behive under the heat of the sun. "Cool-ade, cool-ade . . . lemon, pineapple, *jamaica,* young man. . ." The age-old wail of the lame and dark Indian woman, "chicuilotiii . . . tos . . . fritos[8] . . . and the delirious flute of the grinder. . . . (I, 574)

After *La Luciérnaga* Azuela abandoned this distorted manner of writing and returned to the style of his first period. The main reason for this backward leap, as the novelist said, was that he wanted to write for the average reader and not for a select few:

The third novel written with a new technique is called *La Luciér-naga* and it has been the greatest literary success I have had in my life, as well as the most dismal economic failure. Published by Espasa Calpe of Madrid nineteen years ago [. . .], of the two thousand copies printed more than a thousand remain in their warehouse. That fact causes me more grief than the joy I received upon hearing the applause of the men of letters. Not that I regret, either, the money I do not earn [. . .], but the fact that the book does not sell, since I have always recognized myself as being a popular novelist who writes for the general public and not for men of letters. What I am most interested in when I write a book is that it be read by the largest possible number of readers. (III, 1117, 1118)

The novels Azuela wrote after *La Luciérnaga,* in which he used a straightforward style, often writing carelessly, do not add anything to his stature as a stylist or as a novelist. With the possible exception of *Nueva burguesía,* these novels present no novelty whatsoever. Azuela did not want to imitate the style of the new writers and preferred to compose in the manner of his early periods. He did not believe, to be sure, that it was necessary to introduce stylistic innovations in order to write a great novel. This concept of the novel, it seems, was derived from the great English novelist W. Somerset Maugham, whom Azuela quotes in order to strengthen his own idea. "There doesn't exist a good novel," said Maugham, "in which it is not necessary to be rather simple in order that any person of average culture and intelligence may read it with ease. The style must also be good, notwithstanding the fact that the four greatest novelists of the world, Balzac, Tolstoy, Dickens, and Dostoevski were mediocre writers of their own language." [9]

Although there are pronounced differences in the style of the four groups of novels that Azuela wrote, certain characteristics that recur frequently give continuity to his development as a writer. Some of these characteristics have already been mentioned: the use of words peculiar to the Spanish of Mexico; the predominance of dialogue over description; the quick brushstroke of words to paint a scene; the short, staccato sentence to give his style a nervous, dynamic impact. Other characteristics peculiar to his style are the use of certain key words, of images that reflect an interest in his native soil, of metaphors based on the association of the several levels of life (animal, vegetable, human), and a very personal use of certain adjectives. His style, it can be said, reflects his personal interests, his personal likes and dislikes, and his preoccupations in life, which were centered around rural Mexico, medicine, and life among the poor city dwellers.

The influences of his profession upon his style can be found in the use of medical terminology and in the creation of images derived from that field. He often speaks about voices that have a cold, of eyes that are vitrified, of consumptive thick lips, of mangy pity, of neurotic asceticism, of semi-idiotic happiness. Figures of speech are often derived from the field of medicine: a guitar sheds nitroglycerine tears, Factor Street is compared to an enormous esophagus, and the *pitahayo* plant has branches like the fingers of a giant suffering from ankylosis.

For Azuela, a writer's style must be effective enough to hold the attention of the reader, to make him feel with the characters and identify himself with them. Azuela's style is powerful enough to accomplish all this and more. He had, indeed, the magic touch necessary to hold the reader's attention and make him live in another world, even one as unattractive as that found in his novels about life in the slums of Mexico City.[10]

CHAPTER 9

Concluding Remarks

THE literature of the Mexican Revolution is the result of historical events that affected the lives of each individual and changed the face of Mexico. The revolutionary movement which began in 1910 and ended about 1940 was a struggle against the Díaz feudal regime and its social institutions. The new program favored a democratic form of government, social justice, land reforms, and a more equitable distribution of wealth. This struggle provided writers with materials to compose novels, short stories, memoirs, dramas, and poems in which they gave expression to the ideals of the revolution without overlooking the tremendous loss of lives, destruction of property, and human suffering. This body of writing soon came to be known as the literature of the Mexican Revolution. Its initiator and best exponent was Mariano Azuela.

The literature of the revolution, whether in the narrative, dramatic, or lyric form, has something in common besides subject matter. It breaks completely with the past and rejects the esthetic ideas of the *modernistas,* who were mainly interested in creating exotic worlds while ignoring their immediate environment and the problems of the society of which they formed a part. At the same time, it does not imitate the forms prevalent in Europe at the time, which do appear in the works of the avant-garde writers.

Those writers identified with the revolutionary movement produced a social literature that reflects the world in which they lived, a literature that does not ignore, as do the works of the *modernistas* first and the *vanguardistas* later, Mexico's real problems. Alongside an art in which pure form prevailed, they placed one in which the contents are vital and dramatic and of interest to all the people, for it gives expression to their struggle on the battlefield, in the towns, and in the city halls.

The heroes of the writers of the revolution are no longer Chinese princesses, fallen angels, or refined upper-class idle young men; on the contrary, they are common soldiers and their wives, persecuted farmers, and suffering peons. This new subject matter determined the use of more appropriate forms and a new style, which is often abrupt, choppy and even disrupted, as the revolution itself.

The theme of the revolution, although it does appear in drama and in poetry, is better expressed in the narrative forms, especially the novel. The creator of this sub genre is, as has been so often stated, Mariano Azuela, author of the first (*Andrés Pérez, maderista,* 1911) and best (*Los de abajo,* 1915) novels of the Mexican Revolution. His influence upon other novelists of the revolution, and indeed upon post revolutionary novelists, cannot be overestimated.

Reading the novels of Azuela is a rewarding experience. In them the reader finds not only the portrait of a country in transition but also absorbing stories well told, for Azuela was a born novelist. He had the ability to make the reader identify with his characters and to censure, or sympathize with, their ambitions and weaknesses. Azuela's world is a contemporary one, beset with innumerable social and political problems, but the novelist never turns his back on those problems, and he never turns away from those of the common people. Reading Azuela's novels is the best way to get a profile of modern Mexico and the best way to become acquainted with the Mexican people, of which he himself was an excellent representative. But the reader gets much more than that. He is left with the impression that the novel he has just read has not only increased his knowledge of Mexico but has also enriched him spiritually. He has come in contact with the mind of a narrator who could project his ideals into his works of fiction, and who dedicated his life to make his nation a better place in which to live.

Notes and References

Chapter One

1. Mariano Azuela, *Obras completas*, 3 vols. (Mexico: Fondo de Cultura Económica, vols. I and II, 1958; vol. III, 1960), III, 1126. My translation, as in the following quotations from this work. References to this edition, not footnoted, are indicated by volume and page number only.
2. *Ibid.*
3. *Ibid.,* p. 1127.
4. *Ibid.,* pp. 1127–28.
5. *Ibid.,* pp. 1112–77.
6. *Cf. ibid.,* III, 1127, and II, 721.
7. *Ibid.,* III, 1197–1236.
8. As stated in an interview with José Pichel published in the review *Claridades literarias* (Mexico City, May 7, 1959), p. 5.
9. *Obras completas,* III, 813.
10. *Ibid.,* p. 814.
11. *Ibid.,* p. 845.
12. *Ibid.,* p. 1048.
13. See Alfonso de Alba, *Antonio Moreno y Oviedo y la Generación de 1903.* Prólogo de Mariano Azuela (Mexico, 1949), and Allen W. Phillips, *Francisco González León* (Mexico: Instituto Nacional de Bellas Artes, 1964).
14. Translated into English by Anita Brenner under the title *Marcela; A Mexican Love Story* (New York: Farrar and Rinehart, 1932).
15. *Obras completas,* III, 1070.
16. *Ibid.*
17. *Ibid.,* p. 1075.
18. *Ibid.,* pp. 1075–76.
19. *Ibid.,* p. 1079.
20. *Ibid.,* p. 1087. This last scene, the death of Demetrio Macías, is one of the most beautiful in the novel.
21. *Ibid.,* pp. 1081–82.
22. *Ibid.,* p. 1076.
23. *Ibid.*

24. English translation by Lesley B. Simpson, with *Los caciques: Two Novels of Mexico: The Flies, The Bosses* (Los Angeles: University of California Press, 1956).

25. *Ibid.,* p. 1112.

26. See John E. Englekirk, "The Discovery of *Los de abajo* by Mariano Azuela," *Hispania,* XVIII (1935), 53–62.

27. Translated by Enrique Munguía, Jr. Illustrations by José Clemente Orozco. The second English edition appeared in London, published by Jonathan Cape in 1930. A reprint of the Brentano's edition has been issued in paperback by Signet (1962) with a Foreword by Harriet de Onís. A new translation, using the same title, is that of Frances Kellam Hendrick and Beatrice Berler, *Two Novels of the Mexican Revolution: The Trials of a Respectable Family, The Underdogs* (San Antonio, Texas: Principia Press of Trinity University, 1963).

28. Translated by Joaquín Maurín. It appeared between Nov. 17, 1928, and March 16, 1929.

29. *Obras completas,* III, 1077.

30. The second was *El desquite* (1925), the least successful of the three.

31. *Obras completas,* III, 1118.

32. As stated in the interview with Pichel (see Note 8).

33. *Obras completas,* III, 1175.

34. *Obras completas,* III, 1176.

35. *Ibid.,* p. 1192.

Chapter Two

1. English translation by Katherine Anne Porter under the title *The Itching Parrot* (Garden City, New York: Doubleday, Doran, and Company, 1942).

2. Consult Jefferson Rea Spell, *The Life and Works of José Joaquín Fernández de Lizardi* (Philadelphia: University of Pennsylvania Press, 1931).

3. English translation by Harvey L. Johnson, *Christmas in the Mountains* (Gainesville: University of Florida Press, 1961).

4. See Robert J. Niess, "Zola's *L'Oeuvre* and *Reconquista* of Gamboa," *PMLA,* LXI (1946), 577–83.

5. *Obras completas,* III, 1012–13. Azuela was in his fifth year of the study of medicine in 1897.

6. *Ibid.,* p. 1025.

7. *Ibid.,* p. 687.

8. *Ibid.,* p. 1276.

9. The principal studies about the novel in Mexico before Azuela

are those of John S. Brushwood, *The Romantic Novel in Mexico* (Columbia, Missouri, 1955); Joaquina Navarro, *La novela realista mexicana* (Mexico, 1955); Ralph E. Warner, *Historia de la novela mexicana en el siglo XIX* (Mexico, 1953); John L. Read, *The Mexican Historical Novel, 1826–1910* (New York, 1939); also the first part of J. S. Brushwood and José Rojas Garcidueñas, *Breve historia de la novela mexicana* (Mexico, 1959).

10. *María Luisa* (Lagos de Moreno: Imprenta López Arce, 1907); the second edition did not appear until 1938: *María Luisa y otros cuentos* (Mexico, Andrés Botas, editor); and the third is the one included in the *Obras completas*, II, 707–63.

11. *María Luisa y otros cuentos* (Mexico, 1938), pp. 8–9.

12. *Ibid.*, pp. 21–22.

13. *Ibid.*, p. 160.

14. The first edition appeared in Mexico City in 1908, printed by Müller Brothers; the second edition, also published in Mexico City, has the date 1918; a third edition was published in the newspaper *El Nacional* in 1933, and a fourth by Botas in Mexico City. The fifth and last is the one included in the *Obras completas*, I, 3–112.

15. *Obras completas*, III, 1046.

16. *Ibid.*

17. *Ibid.*, I, 66.

18. English translation by Ethel Brinton, under the title *The Edge of the Storm* (Austin: University of Texas Press, 1963).

19. An important review of *Los fracasados* not mentioned by Azuela is the one that appeared in the literary review *El Cojo Ilustrado* of Bogotá, Colombia, XVIII (1909), 339.

20. The first edition was published in Guadalajara, in the Talleres de *La Gaceta de Guadalajara* in 1909. The second did not appear until 1924, in Mexico City, printed by Rosendo Terrazas. The third (1937) and fourth (1945) were printed by Botas in Mexico City. The fifth is the one in the *Obras completas*, I, 113–224.

21. *Obras completas*, III, 1056.

22. Gregorio Ortega, "Azuela dijo . . .," *El Universal Ilustrado*, Mexico City (January 29, 1925).

23. This story was translated by the ethnologist Frederick Starr and included in his book *Readings from Modern Mexican Authors* (Chicago: The Open Court Publishing Company, 1904).

24. *Obras completas*, I, 130.

25. For a study of the Spanish spoken in Azuela's native State see Daniel N. Cárdenas, "El español de Jalisco (Contribución a la geografía lingüística hispanoamericana)," *Orbis*, III (1954), 62–67.

26. *Obras completas*, I, 224.

27. First ed. printed by Müller Hnos.; 2nd ed. by Botas, 1945; 3rd ed. *Obras completas*, I, 225–319.

28. *Ibid.*, III, 1064.

29. *Ibid.*, pp. 1063–64.

30. *Ibid.*, I, 269–70.

31. *Ibid.*, III, 1064.

Chapter Three

1. The first edition was printed in Mexico City and edited by Blanco and Botas in 1911. A copy of this rare first edition may be consulted at the New York Public Library. The second edition did not appear until 1945, in Mexico City, edited by Botas. The third edition is that included in the *Obras completas*, II, 764–800.

2. The first edition was published in Mexico City in 1917 by the Talleres Editoriales de la Compañía Periodística Nacional, of the newspaper *El Universal*. The second edition appeared the same year and was published by the newspaper *El Nacional*. The third edition is that of *La Razón*, 1931. The fourth is that included in the anthology edited by Antonio Castro Leal, *La novela de la Revolución Mexicana* (Mexico, 1958), pp. 69–114, and the fifth, the one of *Obras completas*, II, 801–66.

3. *Obras completas*, II, 828.

4. *Ibid.*, 824.

5. The first edition is the one published by the newspaper *El Paso del Norte*, El Paso, Texas, between October and December, 1915; (2nd ed., El Paso, Texas: Imprenta de *El Paso del Norte*, 1916); the twenty-fourth edition is published by the Fondo de Cultura Económica, Mexico City, in 1960. It appears in Vol. I of the *Obras completas*, pp. 320–419, as the twenty-third edition. For other editions see Luis Leal, *Mariano Azuela, vida y obra* (Mexico, 1961), pp. 135–36.

6. *Obras completas*, I, 38.

7. *Ibid.*, II, 1041. In the State of Jalisco and others in the Central region of Mexico, due to the earth's high mineral contents, the water in springs often has a blue tinge. This image of "blue water" is common in Azuela's prose. In Guadalajara the most famous public park has the name "Parque Agua Azul." Famous also are the blue glass objects manufactured in Jalisco.

8. *Obras completas*, I, 329.

9. Is it a coincidence that in Azuela's home in Lagos there was a servant called Camila?

10. *Obras completas*, I, 329: "Cuando atardeció en llamaradas que tiñeron el cielo en vivísimos colores, pardearon unas casuchas en una explanada, entre las montañas azules. Demetrio hizo que lo llevaran allí."

11. *Ibid.,* p. 352: "Todos ensanchaban sus pulmones como para respirar los horizontes dilatados, la inmensidad del cielo, el azul de las montañas y el aire fresco, embalsamado de las aromas de la sierra. Y hacían galopar sus caballos, como si en aquel correr desenfrenado pretendieran posesionarse de toda la tierra."

12. *Ibid.,* p. 393: "Era un amanecer silencioso y de discreta alegría. Un tordo piaba tímidamente en el fresno; los animales removían la basura del rastrojo en el corral; gruñó un cerdo su somnolencia. Asomó el tinte anaranjado del sol, y la última estrellita se apagó."

13. *Ibid.,* p. 418: "El humo de la fusilería no acaba de extinguirse. Las cigarras entonan su canto imperturbable y misterioso; las palomas cantan con dulzura en las rinconadas de las rocas; ramonean apaciblemente las vacas.

La sierra está de gala; sobre sus cúspides inaccesibles cae la niebla albísima como un crespón de nieve sobre la cabeza de la novia.

Y al pie de una resquebrajadura enorme y suntuosa como pórtico de vieja catedral, Demetrio Macías, con los ojos fijos para siempre, sigue apuntando con el cañón del fusil . . ."

14. *Ibid.,* I, 351.

15. This first story was first published in *Obras completas,* II, 1070–75. All these works will be discussed individually.

16. The first edition appeared in Mexico City, printed by the Tip. de A. Carranza e Hijos in 1918; 2nd ed., México: Ediciones de La Razón, 1931; 3rd ed., in Antonio Castro Leal (ed.), *La novela de la Revolución Mexicana* (Madrid, 1958), pp. 115–55; 4th ed., *Obras completas,* II, 867–925. English translation by Lesley B. Simpson, *Two Novels of Mexico: The Flies, The Bosses* (Los Angeles: University of California Press, 1956).

17. *Obras completas,* II, 913.

18. "Domitilo Wants to Be a Congressman." The first edition, together with *Las moscas* and *De cómo al fin lloró Juan Pablo,* was published in Mexico City in 1918 by A. Carranza e Hijos. The second edition, with *Andrés Pérez, maderista* and *De cómo al fin lloró Juan Pablo* is that of Editorial Botas, 1945. The 3rd ed. is the one included in *Obras completas,* II, 926–50.

19. *Obras completas,* II, 1070–75. This is the only publication of this story.

20. *Ibid.,* p. 940.

21. The first ed. appeared in the newspaper *El Mundo* of Tampico, Tamaulipas, in 1918; the second edition was also published by this newspaper; 3rd ed., México: Ediciones Botas, 1938; 4th ed., México: Ediciones Botas, 1947; 5th ed. *Obras completas,* I, 419–566. English translation: *The Trials of a Respectable Family and the Underdogs,*

by F. K. Hendricks and Beatrice Berler (San Antonio, Texas: Principia Press of Trinity University, 1963).
22. *Obras completas,* I, 484.
23. *Lit.* Citizen First Chief, a title assumed by Venustiano Carranza.
24. *Obras completas,* I, 515.
25. *Ibid.,* III, 570.

Chapter Four

1. See Francisco Monterde, "La etapa del hermetismo en la obra del Dr. Mariano Azuela," *Cuadernos Americanos,* Mexico City (May–June, 1952), pp. 286–88.
2. First edition published by Rosendo Terrazas, Mexico City, 1923; second edition (mutilated) in the review *Contemporáneos,* VIII (1930), 193–216 and IX (1931), 42–70; third edition, Ediciones Botas, 1941; fourth edition, *Obras completas,* II, 951–77.
3. *Obras completas,* II, 954.
4. *Ibid.,* p. 971. "Absurdos también los graves postes de la electricidad. Pasan a lo largo de una calle sobre un caserío mezquino que va empequeñeciéndose hasta lamer el polvo, hasta fundirse en la línea verde gris de la falda de los cerros y allá muy cerca de un cielo como ojo con catarata."
5. See the letter from Azuela to Professor Bernard M. Dulsey as quoted in his article "Azuela Revisited," *Hispania,* XXXV (1952), 331–32.
6. The first edition was published by the literary supplement *El Universal Ilustrado,* Mexico City, in 1925. The second edition, with *La Malhora,* is that of Ediciones Botas, 1941, and the third that of the *Obras completas,* II, 978–1007.
7. The first edition was published by Espasa-Calpe in Madrid and Barcelona in 1932; the second edition appeared in Mexico City in 1955 and was edited by Novaro; the third edition is the one included in the *Obras completas,* I, 567–667.
8. *Obras completas,* I, 657: "Conchita, resuelta hasta la heroicidad, salió en busca de su hija, cerrando, cuanto podía, sus ojos y sus oídos obstinadamente abiertos; atraviesa en zigzag un larguísimo pasillo para evitar las inmundicias regadas por el suelo fangoso, el perro macilento de una vecina de mal genio y peor lengua, el gato que duerme su roña y sus garrapatas, la cieguita que coge el sol a la puerta de su cuarto, el paralítico, entronado en un banco de bolero, entre palomos, gallinas y coconitos ávidos de gusanos y lombrices, que pasa los años viendo, oliendo y maldiciendo. Y ahí encontró a María Cristina, en amena y cordial plática con las astrosas hembras de los lavaderos y vertederos de monstruosas conversaciones: todo lo que puede germinar en un

cerebro primitivo que de la civilización sólo supo asimilar lo más sucio y lo más infame."ᴸ

9. *Obras completas*, I, 665: "Pasan por una esquina donde un grupo de vagos les tiende sus miradas oblicuas. Saltan un caño de agua inmunda donde flotan gatos y perros muertos de tres semanas. Y nadie repara en el cartelón estúpido fijado en un muro: 'Lávese usted las manos para comer.' Atraviesan sin temor por entre los hampones a quienes tanto trabajo cuesta mirar en línea recta, como pronunciar una frase en lengua cristiana. En sus miradas torvas y en sus labios plegados, hay burbujas de odio enconado, de desprecio y de insolencia. Es el mundo de los perros y de los muladares. Perros de todos colores, de todos tamaños y de todas razas. Flacos, mustios, erizos. A muchos les falta una oreja, a otros una pata, los más llevan largas cicatrices en el lomo o en el vientre, de los cuchillos que han probado su filo en ellos. Porque hay gentes humanas, demasiado humanas."

Chapter Five

1. See Bernard Dulsey, "The Mexican Revolution as Mirrored in the Novels of Mariano Azuela," *Modern Language Journal*, XXXV (1951), 385. Also *Obras completas*, III, 1101–2.

2. Emilio Abreu Gómez, "La mitad de la verdad," *Letras de México*, 20 (1 dic., 1937), p. 4.

3. See letter from Azuela to Professor F. M. Kercheville, dated March 16, 1940 and reproduced in *Revista Iberoamericana*, III (1941), 396.

Chapter Six

1. Both novels were first published by the Fondo de Cultura Económica of Mexico City. The only other editions of these last novels are those included in the *Obras Completas de Mariano Azuela*, II (1958), 464–602 and 603–704. Notice of the existence of the manuscript of *Esa sangre* had been given by Mary Nemtzow in her article "*Esa sangre*, una novela inédita del doctor Mariano Azuela," *Revista Iberoamericana*, XIX (1954), 65–70.

Chapter Seven

1. Others claim they were the first to write short stories about the revolution. For a more detailed treatment of this subject see my essay, "La Revolución mexicana y el cuento," in Edmundo Valadés y Luis Leal, *La Revolución y las letras* (México: Instituto Nacional de Bellas Artes, 1960).

2. This story first appeared in his *Obras completas*, II, 1070–75.

3. *Obras completas*, II, 1073: "¿Villa? . . . ¿Carranza? . . .

¿Obregón? . . . X . . . Y . . . Z . . . Doctor, amo la revolución como el volcán que irrumpe; al volcán porque es volcán y a la revolución porque es revolución. Pero las piedras que quedan arriba o abajo después del cataclismo ¿qué me importan a mí?" See also *Los de abajo, Obras completas,* I, 410.

4. "José María," first published in *Bandera de Provincia,* Guadalajara, August 15, 1929; also in *Obras completas,* II, 1094–97.

5. For other stories by Azuela see the Bibliography in my book *Mariano Azuela, vida y obra,* pp. 137–139.

6. One of the several versions of this script was published by Alí Chumacero in vol. III (pp. 512–66) of Azuela's *Obras completas.*

7. Azuela himself talks about González León's criticism of his book in *Obras completas,* III, 1146.

8. "Los críticos nos engañan," *Hoy,* Mexico City, June 29, 1949.

Chapter Eight

1. Xavier Villaurrutia, "Sobre la novela, el relato y el novelista Mariano Azuela," *Rueca,* I, 3 (Invierno, 1942–43), 15.

2. Mariano Azuela, *María Luisa,* 2nd ed. (México: Ediciones Botas, 1938), pp. 155–56.

3. For examples of this type of characterization see *Obras completas,* I, 491, 546, 683, 752, 787, 803; II, 63, 140, 197, 275, 277, 303, 527, 675, 679, 805, 935.

4. See *Obras completas,* I, 235, 660, 695, 699, 705, 767, 771, 914; II, 273, 493, 943.

5. Valéry Larbaud, Prologue to *Ceux d'en bas* (Paris, 1930).

6. For a discussion of the structures of the novels written after *La Luciérnaga* see Luis Leal, *Mariano Azuela . . .,* pp. 128–31.

7. Xavier Villaurrutia, "Sobre la novela, el relato y el novelista Mariano Azuela," p. 16.

8. Until a few years ago Indian women used to sell *chicuilotes* (a kind of wild pigeon now apparently extinct) in the streets of Mexico City and in the markets. They were sold alive in the streets and sometimes fried in the markets, although this was rare. The cry in the streets was "Chicuilotiiii . . . tos . . . viiiivs . . ." (*viiiivs:vivos . . .* alive).

9. As quoted by Azuela in his *Obras completas,* III, 1121.

10. For a more detailed study of Azuela's style see my book, *Mariano Azuela . . .,* pp. 111–22.

Selected Bibliography

PRIMARY SOURCES

For a complete bibliography of Azuela see Luis Leal, *Mariano Azuela, vida y obra* (México: Studium, 1961), pp. 135–68. Here only the first editions of the most important works will be listed. All these works are included in the three-volume edition of his *Obras completas* published in Mexico City by the Fondo de Cultura Económica, vols. I and II in 1958 and vol. III in 1960. With the exceptions noted, all books here listed were published in Mexico City.

I. Novels

María Luisa. Lagos de Moreno: Imprenta López Arce, 1907.
Los fracasados. Tip. y Lit. de Müller Hnos., 1908.
Mala yerba. Guadalajara: Talleres de "La Gaceta de Guadalajara," 1909.
Andrés Pérez, maderista. Imp. de Blanco y Botas, 1911.
Sin amor. Tip. y Lit. de Müller Hnos., 1912.
Los de abajo. Folletín de *El Paso del Norte,* El Paso, Texas, October–December, 1915.
Los caciques. Talleres Editoriales de la Cía. Periodística Nacional, 1917.
Las moscas. Tip. de A. Carranza e Hijos, 1918.
Domitilo quiere ser diputado. Tip. de A. Carranza e Hijos, 1918.
Las tribulaciones de una familia decente. Folletín de *El Mundo,* Tampico, Tamaulipas, 1918.
La Malhora. Imp. y Encuad. de Rosendo Terrazas, 1923.
El desquite. Publicaciones de *El Universal Ilustrado,* 1925.
La luciérnaga. Madrid-Barcelona: Espasa-Calpe, S.A., 1932.
Pedro Moreno, el insurgente. In *El Nacional,* from December 4, 1933 to March 4, 1934.
Precursores. Santiago de Chile: Ercilla, 1935.
El camarada Pantoja. Editorial Botas, 1937.
San Gabriel de Valdivias, comunidad indígena. Santiago de Chile: Ercilla, 1938.
Regina Landa. Editorial Botas, 1939.

Avanzada. Editorial Botas, 1940.
Nueva burguesía. Buenos Aires: Club del Libro A.L.A., 1941.
La marchanta. Secretaría de Educación Pública, 1944.
La mujer domada. El Colegio de México, 1946.
Sendas perdidas. Editorial Botas, 1949.
La maldición. Fondo de Cultura Económica, 1955.
Esa sangre. Fondo de Cultura Económica, 1956.

II. Short Stories

"Impresiones de un estudiante," *Gil Blas Cómico,* Mexico City, March 5, August 24, September 14, 28, October 12, 26, and November 22, 1896. Signed "Beleño."
"De mi tierra," *El Imparcial,* June, 1903.
"Víctimas de la opulencia," *El Defensor del Pueblo,* Lagos de Moreno, October, 1904. Signed "X."
"En derrota," *El Imparcial,* 1904.
"Avichuelos negros," *Ocios literarios,* III (1909), 15–24.
"De como al fin lloró Juan Pablo," *Revista Universal,* New York, June 15, 1918.
"El jurado," *El Hombre,* I, Number 9, April 9, 1922.
"Y ultimadamente . . ." *Antena,* IV, October, 1924, pp. 4–5.
"Un rebelde," *La Espera,* Madrid, 1929.
"José María," *Bandera de Provincia,* Guadalajara, August 15, 1929.
"La nostalgia de mi coronel," *Hoy,* Number 33, October 9, 1937, p. 25.
"Anuncios a línea desplegada," *Hoy,* Number 41, December 4, 1937, p. 28.
"Era un hombre honrado," *La Nación,* Buenos Aires, January 1, 1940.
"¡Tal será la voluntad de Dios!" *Hoy,* Number 50, February 5, 1938.

III. Theater, Biography, and Criticism

Los de abajo; El buho en la noche; Del Llano Hermanos, S. en C. Ediciones Botas, 1938.
El padre Agustín Rivera. Ediciones Botas, 1942.
Cien años de novela mexicana. Ediciones Botas, 1947.
Epistolario y archivo. Universidad Nacional Autónoma de México, 1969. Letters from and to Azuela edited by Beatrice Berler. Adds little to what we already know about Azuela's life.

IV. Translations (English only)

The Underdogs. [*Los de abajo*]. Translated by Enrique Munguía, Jr. Preface by Carleton Beals. Illustrations by José Clemente Orozco.

New York: Brentano's, 1929. Second ed., London: Jonathan Cape, 1930. Third ed., paperback, with Foreword by Harriet de Onís, New York: Signet Classics, 1962.

Marcela; a Mexican Love Story. [*Mala yerba*]. Translated by Anita Brenner. Introduction by Waldo Frank. New York: Farrar and Rinehart, 1932.

Two Novels of Mexico: The Flies, The Bosses. [*Las moscas; Los caciques*]. Translated by Lesley B. Simpson. Los Angeles: University of California Press, 1956.

Two Novels of the Mexican Revolution: The Trials of a Respectable Family; The Underdogs. Translated by F. K. Hendricks and Beatrice Berler. San Antonio, Texas: Principia Press of Trinity University, 1963.

SECONDARY SOURCES

AZUELA, SALVADOR. "De la vida y del pensamiento de Mariano Azuela," *Revista Universidad de México*, VI, 66 (June, 1952), 3, 29. Comments upon the life and thought of Azuela by his son.

BAIRD, PEGGY. "*Marcela*," *New Republic*, LXXIII (1932), 143. Brief review of *Mala yerba*.

BLOM, FRANS. "*The Underdogs*," *Saturday Review of Literature*, VI (1929), 179. Brief review of *Los de abajo*.

BRENNER, ANITA. "Blood and Struggle of Mexico Incarnate in *Underdogs*," *New York Evening Post* (August 31, 1929). Perceptive review of *Los de abajo*.

DULSEY, BERNARD M. "The Mexican Revolution as Mirrored in the Novels of Mariano Azuela," *Modern Language Journal*, XXXV (1951), 382–86. Summary of Ph.D. thesis tracing the Revolution in the novels of Azuela.

ENGLEKIRK, JOHN E. "The discovery of *Los de abajo* by Mariano Azuela," *Hispania*, XVIII (1935), 53–62. Summary of events leading to the discovery of Azuela's novel by Francisco Monterde.

————. "Mariano Azuela: A Summing Up (1873–1952)," *South Atlantic Studies for Sturgis E. Leavitt*. Washington, D.C., 1953, pp. 127–35. Excellent résumé.

EVANS, ERNESTINE. "In the Days of Díaz: *Marcela* by Mariano Azuela," *New York Herald Tribune Book Review* (September 25, 1932), p. 8. Brief review of *Mala yerba*.

FRANK, WALDO. "*The Underdogs*," *The New Republic*, LX (October 23, 1929), pp. 275–76. Review of *Los de abajo* showing keen insight.

GANNETT, LEWIS. "*The Underdogs*," *The New York Herald Tribune Book Review* (August 25, 1929). Also in *Mexican Life*, V (September, 1929), under title "A Realistic Chronicle of the Revolution."

GOLDBERG, ISAAC. "The Underdogs," *The New World Monthly,* I (January, 1930), 66–68. Excellent review of *Los de abajo.*

GRUENING, ERNEST. *"The Underdogs," The Nation,* CXXIX (1929), 689–90. Well-informed review by the author of *Mexico and Its Heritage.*

GUERRA, MANUEL H. *"La maldición," Books Abroad,* XXX (1956), 288. Short review.

————. *"Esa sangre," Books Abroad,* XXXI (1957), 408. Short review. Halperin, Maurice. *"Pedro Moreno, el insurgente," Books Abroad,* X (1936), 468. Knowledgeable review.

HURTADO, ALFREDO. *Mariano Azuela, novelista de México.* Guadalajara: Xallixtlico, 1951. 21 pages. Brief but good essay on Azuela.

IDUARTE, ANDRÉS. "La mujer domada," *Revista Hispánica Moderna,* XIII (1947), 59–60. One of the few reviews dedicated to this novel.

JONES, DEWEY R. *El doctor Mariano Azuela, médico y novelista.* México: Universidad Nacional Autónoma de México, 1960. M.A. thesis; rich in biographical information obtained from Azuela's archives.

KERCHERVILLE, FRANCIS M. "El liberalismo de Azuela," *Revista Iberoamericana,* III (1941), 381–98. An interpretation of Azuela's ideology.

LEAL, LUIS. *Mariano Azuela, vida y obra.* México: Studium, 1961.

LUCKEY, ROBERT E. "Mariano Azuela: 1873–1952," *Books Abroad,* XXVII (1953), 368–70. A good summing-up.

MALAGAMBA URIARTE, ANGÉLICA. *La novela de Mariano Azuela.* México: Universidad Nacional Autónoma de México, 1951. M.A. thesis.

MONTERDE, FRANCISCO. *En defensa de una obra y de una generación.* México: Imprenta Universitaria, 1935. Contains a translation of Englekirk's article "The discovery of *Los de abajo*" and the three articles by Monterde on which it is based.

NICHOLS, MADALINE W. *"La luciérnaga," Books Abroad,* VIII (1934), 459–60. Brief review.

OWEN, ARTHUR. *"Los de abajo," Books Abroad,* V (1931), 264–65. Short review.

PACHECO, JOSÉ EMILIO. *"La mujer domada," Estaciones,* Mexico City, II, 7 (1957), 362–63. Short review pointing out the defects in the novel.

PALACIOS, EMMANUEL. *Mariano Azuela: un testimonio literario.* Guadalajara, 1952. Brief (24 pages) but excellent essay.

————. *Mariano Azuela y su obra.* Los Altos, Jalisco, 1954. Perceptive study.

PICHEL, JOSÉ. "Viendo actuar a Azuela . . ." *Claridades literarias,* Mexico City, May 7, 1959, p. 5. Interview with Azuela's widow.

RODRÍGUEZ MONEGAL, EMIR. "Mariano Azuela y la novela de la Revolución Mexicana," *Narradores de esta América.* [Barcelona], *n.d.,* pp. 21–34. Also pp. 35–38. Interpretation of the Mexican novelist by Uruguay's outstanding contemporary critic.

SELVA, MAURICIO DE LA. "*Obras completas,*" *Cuadernos Americanos,* XVIII, ciii, 2 (1959), 271–73. Brief review.

SPELL, J. R. "Mexican Society of the Twentieth Century as Portrayed by Mariano Azuela," *Inter American Intellectual Interchange.* Austin, Texas: University of Texas Press, 1943, pp. 49–61. Documented study of Azuela's milieu.

TORRES-RÍOSECO, ARTURO. "Mariano Azuela (1873)," *Revista Cubana,* XI, 31 (1938), 44–72. One of the first studies dedicated to Azuela.

TYRE, CARL A. "*El camarada Pantoja,*" *Books Abroad,* XII (1938), 361–62. Brief review.

VALADÉS, EDMUNDO. "*La maldición* de Azuela," *Novedades,* Mexico City, July 12, 1955. Azuela as interpreted by a writer of a younger generation.

WALSH, DONALD D. "*La mujer domada,*" *Books Abroad,* XXI (1947), 300. Brief review.

WOOLSEY, A.W. "Los protagonistas de algunas novelas de Mariano Azuela," *Hispania,* XXIII (1940), 341–48. A partial study of Azuela's protagonists.

Index

Books that have been translated are listed under their English titles, if such titles are mentioned in the text.